HOW TO STOP BEING TOXIC:

BREAK FREE FROM MANIPULATIVE HABITS, PROTECT YOUR LOVED ONES, AND BUILD HEALTHIER RELATIONSHIPS

W. B. SMITH

INTRODUCTION

There was a time when I sat across from a friend who was visibly upset. Her eyes, usually bright and full of life, were clouded with hurt. She came to me to discuss a recent argument with her partner. As she spoke, I realized that her story was not unlike many others I had heard. Words that should have conveyed love had turned sharp like daggers. Misunderstandings had spiraled into a pattern of blame and defensiveness. It was a moment that emphasized the transformative power of toxic behaviors, turning what should be moments of love and understanding into hurt and conflict in our closest relationships.

My journey toward understanding and changing toxic habits began in my early years. I have always had a passion for helping others. I found myself drawn to the complexities of human relationships. I wanted to understand why we sometimes hurt the ones we love and, more importantly, how to stop. This passion has led me here to write this book for you. I aim to lead you toward healthier, more fulfilling relationships.

The purpose of this book is clear. It is designed to provide actionable steps to recognize and change toxic habits. It will help you protect your loved ones and build healthier relationships. You deserve to live free from the destructive patterns that can hold you back. Together, we will explore how to make meaningful changes that last.

If you find yourself struggling with relationships, this book is for you. You might feel trapped by habits you wish you could change. Or you might be looking for ways to connect more deeply with those you care about. Whatever your situation, I want you to know that I understand your struggles and aspirations. This book is crafted with your needs in mind.

You will find a roadmap to transformation. We will dive into self-reflection, emotional regulation, communication, and empathy. Each chapter will offer insights and strategies to help you navigate these areas. By the end, you will better understand yourself and your relationships.

Addressing toxic behavior often comes from a desire for personal growth. You want to repair relationships or achieve emotional stability. These are powerful motivators, and this book will guide you through these changes. You will learn how to transform your interactions and create positive dynamics.

What sets this book apart is its commitment to practical, actionable solutions. You will walk away with tangible tools to implement positive life changes. Each chapter includes exercises and real-life examples to help you apply what you learn.

This book takes a holistic approach and focuses on empathy development as a key to transformation. You will discover how understanding and compassion can change how you relate to others and yourself. It is about stopping toxic behaviors and embracing a healthier lifestyle.

I encourage you to commit to this journey of self-improvement and relationship healing. Engage deeply with the content and apply the insights and strategies provided. Change is not always easy, but it is possible with dedication and effort.

As you turn the pages, I hope you feel a sense of hope and possibility. You have the power to transform your life and relationships. Embrace the process of growth and change. The path to a healthier, more fulfilling life is within your reach. Let's begin this journey together.

CHAPTER 1
UNDERSTANDING TOXICITY: THE FOUNDATION

While scrolling through social media one evening, I stumbled upon an intense debate. Friends were arguing, and as the comments piled up, the air became thick with accusations and defensiveness. It was clear that something deeper was at play—not just about differing opinions. What I witnessed was a microcosm of toxic interactions that affect many of us, often without our conscious awareness. These interactions disrupt our lives, damage relationships, and leave us wondering how things got so out of control. This chapter aims to dismantle the layers of toxicity that can seep into our behaviors and interactions, helping you recognize and address them in your own life.

Defining Toxicity: Beyond the Buzzword

In today's world, "toxic" is thrown around quite frequently. Yet, it's crucial to grasp its true meaning, especially when discussing personal behaviors and interactions. Toxicity is not merely about having a bad day or feeling stressed. It's about persistent patterns that harm ourselves and others. These patterns might manifest as manipulation, constant criticism, or refusal to take responsibility for one's actions. Unlike temporary negativity everyone experiences, these behaviors are consistent and damaging. Understanding this difference is the first step in recognizing when toxicity is at play in our lives.

A common misconception is that labeling someone as "toxic" means they are inherently bad. This is not accurate. Toxicity refers to behaviors, not the entirety of a person. Everyone has the capacity for growth and change. Addressing and altering specific behaviors is vital rather than dismissing individuals altogether. This distinction is important because it opens the door to self-awareness and improvement. It allows for a compassionate approach where we can understand and modify our actions without harsh self-judgment.

Interestingly, some toxic behaviors can appear functional, especially in specific environments. For instance, a highly competitive workplace might reward aggressive tactics that are considered toxic in personal relationships. Similarly, high-stress situations may trigger coping mechanisms that, while seemingly beneficial in the short term, become harmful if they spill over into other areas of life. It's essential to recognize when these behaviors cross the line from being situationally appropriate to personally destructive.

Cultural backgrounds also play a significant role in shaping perceptions of toxicity. What one culture views as assertive, another might see as aggressive. Social norms and expectations can influence how behaviors are interpreted and whether they are acceptable or toxic. It's essential to consider these cultural nuances when evaluating behavior. This awareness helps us understand the context of our actions and those of others, promoting empathy and reducing misjudgments.

Reflection Exercise: Recognize Your Patterns

Take a moment to reflect on your interactions over the past week. Have you noticed any recurring behaviors that might be harmful or misunderstood? Consider how these actions fit into the patterns we've discussed. Write down any thoughts or insights that come to mind. This exercise can be a starting point for deeper exploration into your behaviors and how they might impact your relationships. Reflecting in writing can help clarify your thoughts and encourage honesty with yourself.

Understanding toxicity is not about self-blame or guilt. It's about gaining clarity and taking the first steps toward positive change. By identifying and addressing these patterns, you can transform your relationships and create a more supportive and loving environment for yourself and those around you. The process requires patience and self-compassion, but the rewards are profound. You can change the narrative and build healthier, more fulfilling relationships.

The Roots of Toxic Behavior: From Childhood to Adulthood

The roots of toxic behavior often stretch deep into the soil of our formative years, where childhood experiences and family dynamics lay the groundwork for how we relate to the world. Imagine a young child observing their parents' interactions. These moments can profoundly shape the child's understanding of how relationships work. If a child witnesses constant criticism or manipulation between parents, they may internalize these behaviors as normal. This is the essence of parental modeling—the behaviors we see in our caregivers often become the blueprint for our future interactions. When neglect or trauma enters the picture, the impact can be even more profound.

A child who feels unsafe or unloved may develop defensive mechanisms that later manifest as toxic behaviors. This is a survival strategy to cope with an environment that lacks stability or affection.

As we grow, we continue to learn behaviors from those around us. This concept of learned behaviors highlights the powerful influence of our social circles. Have you ever noticed how a group of friends might all have similar ways of handling conflict? This is no accident. We often imitate those we spend the most time with, adopting their habits and attitudes. If the group reinforces these behaviors—perhaps through laughter or acceptance—they become ingrained. Over time, these learned behaviors can harden into toxic patterns, especially if they are never questioned or challenged. The reinforcement loop of social approval can make it difficult to recognize when these behaviors are problematic.

Insights from developmental psychology provide a deeper understanding of how these behaviors evolve. One key concept is attachment styles, which are formed in early childhood and influence how we connect with others. Secure attachment, often resulting from consistent and nurturing caregiving, leads to healthier relationships. In contrast, insecure attachment can lead to anxiety and toxic dynamics. Emotional regulation is another crucial aspect of development. As children, we learn to manage our emotions through observation and guidance. Without proper models or support, emotional regulation can become skewed, leading to reactions that others perceive as toxic. A complex interplay of early experiences and ongoing influences shapes how we handle emotions and relationships.

Toxic behaviors can also pass from generation to generation, like a script handed down through familial lines. Intergenerational patterns are common in families where certain behaviors, such as avoidance or aggression, become the norm. Consider a family where silence and withdrawal are the responses to conflict.

These patterns can persist, affecting the immediate family and future generations. Breaking this cycle requires awareness and intention. It's about recognizing these inherited behaviors and making conscious choices to act differently. Case studies of family dynamics often reveal how deeply these patterns can run. Yet, they also show that change is possible. Individuals who commit to self-reflection and growth can shift these patterns, creating a healthier environment for themselves and their descendants.

Reflection Exercise: Identifying Early Influences

Think back to your own childhood experiences and family dynamics. What behaviors did you observe and perhaps adopt? Consider how your early interactions influence your current relationships. Write down any emerging patterns and reflect on how they have shaped your behavior. Recognizing these influences is the first step toward change. Such awareness can guide you in reshaping your interactions and fostering healthier, more supportive relationships. It's about understanding where you've come from to choose where you're going.

Recognizing Toxic Patterns in Daily Life

Identifying toxic patterns in our daily interactions can be a transformative experience. These patterns often manifest through subtle signs that, when overlooked, can lead to significant harm over time. One considerable indicator is manipulative communication. This might appear as someone twisting facts to suit their narrative, using guilt or obligation to sway others, or strategically withholding information to maintain control. For instance, consider a scenario at work where a colleague consistently avoids taking responsibility by shifting blame onto others. Such behavior not only undermines trust but also creates a hostile environment. Another red flag is consistent negativity or criticism, where a person seldom offers praise or validation, instead focusing on faults or shortcomings. This can erode self-esteem and breed resentment. Recognizing these signs is the first step toward addressing and altering them.

Self-reflection is a powerful tool in identifying one's toxic patterns. Engaging in daily journaling prompts can facilitate this process. By writing about your interactions, you can uncover recurring themes and behaviors that might go unnoticed. Questions like, "What triggered my reaction today?" or "How did I communicate my needs?" can illuminate areas for improvement. Reflective questioning techniques encourage deeper introspection, inviting you to explore the motivations behind your actions. This practice promotes self-awareness and empowers you to make conscious changes in how you relate to others. It is a gentle invitation to understand yourself better and to transform your interactions from the inside out.

Seeking external feedback is equally important. Often, we are too close to our behaviors to see them. Others can provide valuable insights into how our actions affect them. Constructive criticism can be a gift when offered in a supportive manner. It differs from judgment, which tends to shut down dialogue and growth. Instead, constructive feedback opens a path for reflection and change. Peer reflections can be particularly enlightening, as friends and colleagues often witness patterns we might be blind to. Their perspectives can serve as a mirror, reflecting the unintended impact of our behavior. Embracing this feedback with an open mind can catalyze meaningful transformation.

Understanding behavioral triggers is crucial in managing toxic behaviors. Stressful situations often act as catalysts, prompting reactions that might otherwise remain dormant. For example, you might use sarcasm or defensiveness during a heated discussion. Recognizing these triggers allows you to anticipate and manage your responses more effectively. Conflict, by its very nature, is a fertile ground for emotional reactions. Whether it's a disagreement with a partner or a misunderstanding with a friend, these moments can escalate if not handled with care. By identifying what triggers your responses—be it a certain tone of voice or a specific topic—you can develop strategies to remain calm and composed. This awareness benefits you and fosters healthier interactions with those around you.

Reflection Exercise: Identifying Red Flags

Take a few minutes daily to jot down interactions that left you unsettled. Look for patterns in communication or emotional responses that stand out. Were there moments when you felt misunderstood or noticed yourself reacting strongly? Reflect on these instances and consider what they reveal about your patterns. This exercise can be valuable in recognizing and altering behaviors that contribute to toxicity in your relationships. By regularly engaging in this practice, you cultivate a habit of self-awareness and proactive change. The journey toward healthier interactions begins with these small, deliberate steps.

The Impact of Toxicity on Relationships and Self-Worth

In relationships, toxic behaviors often create a destructive dance of dependency and control. This can look like a couple where one partner dictates every decision, leaving the other powerless. Over time, the controlled partner may lose their voice, their confidence eroded by the constant dominance of their significant other. This dynamic can extend to friendships and family ties, where one manipulates situations to maintain power or control, often under the guise of care or concern. Emotional manipulation can be subtle, like guilt-tripping a friend into canceling plans to spend time with you, insinuating their absence is a betrayal. While such tactics might achieve short-term goals, they slowly unravel the fabric of trust and respect, turning relationships into battle-grounds of resentment and hurt.

The effect of toxic behaviors on self-perception is profound. Engaging in such behaviors can lead to an internal dialogue filled with negative self-talk. Imagine constantly criticizing yourself for every perceived mistake or shortcoming. This behavior can become a loop, feeding into a cycle of guilt and shame. You might start questioning your worth, feeling undeserving of love and happiness. These feelings can become ingrained, affecting your confidence and ability to engage positively with others. Over time, the weight of these emotions can become overwhelming, leading to a diminished sense of self-worth that colors every interaction.

The long-term consequences of toxicity extend beyond personal relationships, often spilling into professional realms as well. Personal stories have shown how persistent toxic behaviors can lead to the dissolution of long-standing relationships. A friend once shared how their marriage ended after years of unaddressed manipulation and blame. In the workplace, similar patterns can result in career setbacks. Consistent conflict with colleagues or an inability to work collaboratively can stall career advancement. Projects may suffer, and growth opportunities might vanish, leaving you feeling stuck and unfulfilled. The impact is not just external; it is internal, affecting how you see yourself and your potential.

Rebuilding trust after toxicity has damaged a relationship is challenging but not impossible. It begins with accountability—acknowledging the behaviors contributing to the breakdown and taking responsibility for them. This step requires honesty and a willingness to face uncomfortable truths. Change is not immediate; it requires consistent positive actions to demonstrate your commitment to improvement. Open communication, where you actively listen and respond with empathy, can help repair the fractures. Over time, these efforts can rebuild the trust that was lost. It's about creating new patterns, ones that are rooted in respect and mutual understanding.

Rebuilding relationships also involves recognizing the importance of actions aligning with words. Simply stating intentions is not enough. Consistent actions reinforce promises and demonstrate a genuine desire for change. For instance, if you've pledged to be more supportive, showing up for loved ones in meaningful ways will speak volumes. Repetitive positive behavior helps to slowly wash away past hurts and replace them with new, healthier memories. These steps are crucial in mending the bonds that have been strained, allowing relationships to heal and grow stronger.

Common Toxic Traits and How They Manifest

In our interactions, certain toxic traits can quietly weave themselves into the fabric of our daily lives. Two prevalent examples are narcissism and passive-aggressiveness. Individuals with narcissistic tendencies often exude self-centeredness, prioritizing their own needs above others and seeking constant admiration. This can manifest in behaviors like dominating conversations—where one's stories and achievements are always more significant than those of others. It can become exhausting, as those around them might feel unheard and undervalued. Picture a meeting where one person continuously redirects the focus back to their successes, disregarding the contributions of others. This behavior can undermine team morale and stifle collaboration, creating an atmosphere where only one voice truly matters.

Passive aggressiveness, on the other hand, is more insidious. It involves expressing negative feelings indirectly rather than openly. This might include making sarcastic remarks, giving silent treatment, or deliberately dragging one's feet on tasks. Imagine a family gathering where someone consistently makes backhanded compliments, leaving a trail of tension and confusion. These behaviors can erode relationships over time, as the true feelings remain unspoken, yet the sting of their indirect expression lingers. They create an environment where trust is compromised, and genuine communication feels out of reach.

These traits often serve as coping mechanisms for deeper fears and insecurities. Narcissism can be a defense against vulnerability, a way to mask feelings of inadequacy with a facade of superiority. It's a shield to protect against the fear of exposure, of being seen as flawed or weak. Similarly, passive-aggressiveness might stem from an inability to express emotions directly, perhaps due to past experiences where being open led to hurt or rejection. It's a way to assert control when one feels powerless, yet it ultimately creates more barriers than bridges.

Consider the dynamics of office politics, where both traits can thrive. In competitive environments, individuals may undermine others' achievements to advance their standing. A person might downplay a colleague's success in a meeting by subtly suggesting that luck, rather than skill, played a role. This diminishes the colleague's accomplishments and sows discord and suspicion within the team. In social settings, like family events, these traits can turn celebrations into battlegrounds of hidden agendas and unspoken resentments. The pressure to maintain appearances can drive individuals to adopt defensive behaviors, creating a cycle that is difficult to break.

Real-life scenarios offer a window into how these traits play out. In personal relationships, someone might consistently redirect conversations to center around their needs, leaving the other person feeling marginalized. This behavior can diminish the partner's sense of relevance and worth, leading to emotional distance. In professional settings, a team leader who uses passive-aggressive tactics to manage dissent may find their team disengaged, as open communication is stifled. The leader's inability to address issues directly creates an environment where problems fester rather than resolve, impacting productivity and morale.

Understanding the manifestation of these traits is not about assigning blame but recognizing patterns that hinder genuine connection. By acknowledging and addressing these behaviors, we can dismantle the walls they build, replacing them with pathways to understanding and empathy. The journey toward healthier interactions requires us to confront these traits honestly and be willing to change. Only then can we foster relationships grounded in respect and authenticity, where every voice is valued, and every achievement is celebrated.

The Science of Toxicity: Psychological and Emotional Insights

Understanding the psychological roots of toxic behavior is like unraveling a complex tapestry of human cognition and emotion. We see how our thoughts and beliefs shape our actions through the lens of cognitive-behavioral theories. Cognitive-behavioral perspectives suggest that toxic behaviors often stem from distorted thinking patterns. For instance, if someone believes they must always be in control, they might resort to manipulation to maintain that illusion. These distorted thoughts can become habitual, leading to persisting behaviors despite their harmful consequences. Emotional dysregulation theories further illuminate this by explaining how difficulty managing emotions can result in outbursts or passive-aggressive actions. When emotions are not effectively regulated, they can spill over into interactions, creating a cycle of negativity that affects both the individual and those around them.

The emotional toll of toxic behavior is profound. Stress and anxiety are common byproducts, both for the person exhibiting toxic behaviors and for those on the receiving end. Living in an environment where one feels constantly on edge or criticized can lead to chronic stress, affecting mental and physical health. Depression is another potential consequence of toxic environments, as feelings of helplessness and worthlessness take root. The individual exhibiting these behaviors often has an underlying dissatisfaction and unrest as their actions push others away, heightening their isolation. This emotional impact can become a heavy burden, leading to further entrenchment in toxic patterns as a misguided attempt to regain control or validation.

On a neurological level, toxic behaviors can become ingrained through brain patterns and habit formation. With its remarkable plasticity, the brain can adapt to repeated behaviors, making them harder to change. This is where the concept of neuroplasticity becomes critical. Neuroplasticity is the brain's ability to reorganize itself by forming new neural connections. While this ability allows toxic behaviors to become habitual, it also provides hope for change. Individuals can reshape their neural pathways by consciously practicing new, healthier behaviors, gradually reducing the hold of toxic patterns. This scientific insight emphasizes the potential for change with consistent effort and intention.

Therapeutic approaches offer valuable strategies for managing and altering toxic behaviors. Cognitive restructuring techniques help individuals identify and challenge their distorted thinking patterns, replacing them with more balanced perspectives. This process involves introspection and a willingness to confront uncomfortable truths about oneself. Mindfulness and emotional awareness practices are equally powerful. By pursuing mindfulness, individuals learn to observe their thoughts and emotions without judgment, providing a space to respond thoughtfully rather than react impulsively. Emotional awareness enhances one's ability to recognize and name emotions, reducing the likelihood of them manifesting in harmful ways. These therapeutic insights emphasize the importance of self-awareness and intentional action in transforming toxic behaviors.

As we close this exploration of the science behind toxicity, it's important to remember that change is possible. While the path may be challenging, understanding the psychological and emotional underpinnings of toxic behaviors equips us with the knowledge needed to pursue transformation. By embracing cognitive and emotional strategies, we can unravel the patterns that no longer serve us, paving the way for healthier relationships and a more fulfilling life. This journey of change is not just about altering behavior; it is about reclaiming one's life from the shadows of toxicity and stepping into a brighter, more compassionate way of being.

CHAPTER 2

SELF-REFLECTION AND AWARENESS: THE FIRST STEPS

I magine standing on a bustling street, surrounded by the noise of traffic, snippets of conversations, and the chaotic dance of everyday life. Amid this, you feel overwhelmed, unsure of where you're headed. Amidst the noise, there's a quiet voice inside you, often drowned out by the external clamor. This voice is your inner self, waiting to be heard through introspection. Introspection is the deliberate act of examining your thoughts and feelings. It's more than just a casual glance inward; it involves a conscious and honest look at your inner world. It's where you step back and quietly explore what truly matters. Through introspection, you can identify your core values, those guiding principles that define who you are and what you stand for. This process enhances your understanding of yourself and aligns your actions with your deepest values, leading to a more authentic and fulfilling life.

Engaging in self-discovery through introspection has profound benefits. It enhances emotional intelligence by helping you recognize and understand your emotions, and those of others, more clearly. This awareness allows for more empathetic interactions, where you respond rather than react. With greater emotional intelligence, you navigate relationships with grace and understanding, building stronger connections. Additionally, introspection brings greater clarity to your personal goals. It helps you determine what you genuinely want, setting the stage for meaningful achievements that connect with your inner values. Instead of chasing external validation, you pursue goals reflecting your true self, leading to fulfillment and purpose. You can chart a suitable and rewarding course by understanding what drives you.

A variety of techniques can be employed to engage in introspection effectively. Meditation and mindfulness practices are potent tools that foster a state of inner calm and focus. By quieting the mind, you create space for self-reflection, allowing insights to surface naturally. These practices encourage you to observe your thoughts without judgment, fostering a deeper understanding of your mental landscape. Reflective questioning and contemplation are also vital. By asking yourself probing questions, you can uncover the motivations and beliefs that shape your actions. Questions like, "What truly makes me happy?" or "What do I fear the most?" can lead to profound realizations. Contemplation provides the time and space to explore these questions, allowing for insights that can guide personal growth.

Integrating introspection into your daily life can transform how you perceive and interact with the world. Begin with morning reflection rituals, where you set aside a few quiet moments to center yourself. This can involve journaling, meditating, or simply sitting silently, focusing on your breath. These practices help you start the day intentionally and clearly, setting a positive tone for what follows. End-of-day evaluations are equally crucial. As the day winds down, take time to reflect on your experiences. Consider what went well, what challenged you, and how you responded. This practice encourages continuous learning and growth, allowing you to adjust your actions and attitudes to align with your core values.

Reflection Section: Daily Introspection Practice

Consider setting aside five minutes each morning and evening for introspection. In the morning, ask yourself, "What do I want to achieve today?" and in the evening, reflect on, "What did I learn about myself today?" Jot down your thoughts in a journal. Over time, these reflections will reveal patterns and insights, guiding you toward deeper self-awareness and personal growth. This simple practice can become a cornerstone of your journey toward understanding and embracing your authentic self. By committing to this daily routine, you'll cultivate a habit of self-awareness that empowers you to live with intention and purpose.

Identifying Personal Triggers and Emotional Responses

Imagine a moment when your heart races and your palms sweat. A seemingly innocent comment leaves you feeling inexplicably upset. These are emotional triggers at work, powerful stimuli that can provoke intense reactions. Understanding these triggers is vital because they often dictate our emotional responses, sometimes without us even realizing it. Triggers can be situational, like the stress of a crowded room or a looming deadline, or relational, such as a conversation with a friend that touches on past hurts. These moments can catch you off guard, turning a peaceful day into a battleground of emotions. Recognizing what sets you off is the first step in regaining control over your reactions, allowing you to respond with intention rather than reflex.

Mapping your emotional responses to these triggers can be

incredibly enlightening. You might notice a pattern of anger or frustration bubbling when conflict arises. Maybe in high-pressure environments, anxiety takes hold, making it hard to think clearly or act calmly. You understand how different situations affect you by paying attention to these emotional patterns. This awareness allows you to anticipate and prepare to handle your reactions more effectively. Instead of being swept away by emotions, you can pause, reflect, and choose your response, leading to more constructive outcomes.

To identify your triggers, start by keeping a trigger journal. Document moments when you feel a strong emotional response and note common themes or situations that seem to set you off. Over time, patterns will emerge, offering insights into what consistently triggers you. Another helpful strategy is to observe your physical reactions. Often, your body will signal distress before your mind catches up. Pay attention to signs like a tightening chest, clenched jaw, or a racing heart. These physical cues can alert you to the presence of a trigger, giving you a chance to address it before it spirals into a full-blown emotional response. You can manage your triggers more quickly by becoming attuned to these signals.

Once you've identified your triggers, managing and mitigating their impact becomes possible. Developing calming routines can be beneficial. Consider incorporating deep breathing, meditation, or physical exercise into your daily life. These activities can help ground you, providing a sense of calm and control even when faced with a trigger. Establishing safe spaces is another effective strategy. Create environments where you feel secure and at ease, whether in a quiet corner of your home or a favorite natural spot. Retreating to these spaces when you feel overwhelmed can offer the respite you need to regain composure and clarity. By building these routines and spaces into your life, you can cushion the impact of triggers, allowing you to navigate challenging moments with resilience and strength.

Interactive Element: Trigger Journal Exercise

Begin a daily practice of noting your emotional triggers. When you experience an intense reaction, jot down what happened, how you felt, and any physical sensations you noticed. Over time, review your entries to identify recurring themes. Use this insight to anticipate future triggers and develop strategies to manage them. This exercise helps you build a personal roadmap to understanding and mitigating your emotional responses, empowering you to take control of your behavioral patterns and foster healthier interactions. As you continue this practice, your understanding deepens, providing you with the tools to transform your emotional landscape.

Shadow Work: Uncovering Hidden Emotions

Shadow work is a fascinating concept that can illuminate the darker corners of our psyche. Originating from the theories of Carl Jung, shadow work involves examining the hidden or repressed parts of our personality. We often deny or ignore these aspects of ourselves, yet they significantly influence our behavior. Jung described this as the "shadow self," a repository for traits and emotions we find uncomfortable or out of character. Embracing shadow work means acknowledging and integrating these hidden parts into our conscious awareness. Doing so can achieve a more complete and honest understanding of our identity. This process is not about confronting a monster within but rather about reconciling with the parts of ourselves that need attention and healing.

Identifying the shadow self can be challenging, as it often

involves recognizing patterns of self-sabotage, hidden resentments, and deep-seated fears. Self-sabotage might manifest as procrastination or avoidance, actions that prevent us from achieving our goals. These behaviors often stem from a fear of failure or success, as the shadow self seeks to maintain the status quo. Hidden resentments, on the other hand, can linger beneath the surface, subtly influencing our interactions and perceptions. These might emerge as unexplained irritations or grudges, often rooted in unresolved past experiences. Fears, too, can hide within the shadows, influencing our decisions without us even realizing it. By bringing these elements to light, we can understand their origins and reduce their influence on our lives.

Practical exercises can bring hidden emotions to light, making them more manageable and less daunting. Guided visualizations are a powerful tool in this regard. You can invite the shadow self to express itself by visualizing a safe space within your mind. This might involve imagining a dialogue where the shadow speaks, revealing its fears and desires. Such visualizations allow you to explore these emotions without fear, providing insight into their impact on your behavior. Another effective exercise is dialoguing with the shadow self through writing. Set aside time to write a letter to your shadow, asking it questions about its motives and needs. Then, write a response from the shadow's perspective. This dialogue can uncover feelings and beliefs that have long been buried, offering clarity and understanding.

Engaging in shadow work holds transformative potential. One of the most significant benefits is increased self-acceptance. You cultivate a sense of wholeness and acceptance by acknowledging all parts of yourself—the light and the dark. This self-acceptance reduces internal conflict, as you no longer need to hide or deny parts of yourself. Instead, you can embrace your full complexity, recognizing that every trait has positive and negative aspects. This reduction in internal conflict leads to greater peace and harmony as you align your conscious and unconscious selves. It allows you to interact with the world from a place of authenticity and confidence, free from the need to present a curated version of yourself.

Shadowwork also enhances empathy and understanding, both for yourself and others. As you explore your shadow, you gain insight into the hidden motivations and fears driving behavior. This understanding fosters compassion as you realize everyone carries a shadow with them. You become more forgiving of others' shortcomings, recognizing the shared human experience of grappling with hidden emotions. This empathy deepens your connections, allowing for more genuine interactions and relationships. Engaging with your shadow encourages personal growth as you confront the aspects of yourself holding you back. Integrating these repressed parts unlocks potential and creativity, leading to a richer and more fulfilling life.

Journaling for Self-Reflection and Growth

Imagine conversing with yourself—a quiet moment where you lay your thoughts bare without fear of judgment. This is the essence of journaling, an invaluable tool for self-reflection and growth. You record your thoughts and emotions by putting pen to paper, creating a tangible snapshot of your inner world. This practice allows you to express what may be difficult to say aloud and helps track behavioral changes over time. As you revisit past entries, patterns begin to emerge. You might notice how certain situations consistently trigger anxiety or how your emotional responses have evolved. This longitudinal view highlights your progress and illuminates areas that still need attention. Journaling is a mirror, reflecting your journey through personal development and offering insights that might otherwise remain hidden.

Various journaling techniques can cater to different needs and preferences. Stream-of-consciousness writing is a free-form style where you let thoughts flow unchecked onto the page. This method encourages spontaneity and honesty, as there is no right or wrong way to express yourself. It's like opening a valve, allowing emotions and ideas to pour out. On the other hand, prompt-based reflection offers structure, guiding you with specific questions or themes to explore. Prompts can range from introspectively—such as "What are my biggest fears?"—to practical ones, like "What steps can I take today to improve my relationships?" Both methods deepen self-awareness and understanding, providing a safe space to explore your thoughts and feelings without external influence.

Establishing a consistent journaling habit can be transformative but requires intention and commitment. Start by setting a specific time and place for your practice. Whether it's the quiet of dawn or the stillness before sleep, choose a moment that feels right for you. Create an environment conducive to reflection—a cozy nook with a favorite chair or a desk adorned with calming objects. Consistency helps signal to your mind that it's time to turn inward. You might prefer a traditional notebook or explore the convenience of journaling apps that facilitate writing on the go. The key is to choose a medium that feels comfortable and accessible, reducing barriers to regular practice.

Reflective prompts can guide your journaling, offering a starting point when words seem elusive. Consider prompts like, "What am I grateful for today?" to cultivate a mindset of appreciation and positivity. Reflecting on gratitude can shift your perspective, highlighting abundance rather than lack. Another prompt, "Which of my actions today aligned with my core values?" encourages you to evaluate how closely your behavior matches your principles. This reflection fosters accountability and growth as you recognize moments of integrity and identify opportunities for improvement. By regularly engaging with these prompts, you document your thoughts and steer your personal development positively.

Self-Assessment: Are You the Toxic One?

Taking a step back to evaluate your behaviors is crucial in recognizing toxic traits. It requires an objective lens that asks not how you see yourself but how your actions affect those around you. Self-assessment invites honesty, allowing you to see the shadows cast by your behavior. This is not an exercise in self-criticism but an opportunity to understand your impact on others. It's about identifying whether your words and actions build others up or inadvertently tear them down. Through this process, you gain clarity about the dynamics you create in your relationships. Acknowledging these patterns is the first step toward change, leading to healthier interactions and more fulfilling connections.

To begin this self-assessment, consider using specific tools to guide you. Self-assessment questionnaires can be particularly useful. These are structured to prompt reflection on various aspects of your behavior, providing insights into areas like communication styles, emotional responses, and conflict resolution strategies. They can highlight patterns you might have overlooked. Additionally, seeking feedback from trusted individuals offers invaluable perspective. Friends, family, or colleagues can provide insights that you might be too close to see. Their observations can act as a mirror, reflecting the aspects of your behavior that impact them, whether positively or negatively. This feedback should be approached with an open mind and a willingness to listen, even when it feels uncomfortable.

Once you have gathered information through self-assessment,

the next step is interpreting the results. Look for recurring patterns and themes in your behavior. Are there situations where you consistently react in a way that you or others find unhelpful? Identifying these patterns allows you to pinpoint areas for immediate improvement. You may notice a tendency to interrupt others or withdraw in conflicts. Recognizing these tendencies is a powerful realization. It means you are now aware and can begin to take steps toward change. This process of reflection and adaptation can lead to significant personal growth and improved relationships.

Taking responsibility for your actions is a crucial part of this journey. It involves owning your mistakes without slipping into self-condemnation. Acknowledge where you've gone wrong, but do so with the understanding that everyone has flaws and the capacity for change. This acceptance is empowering. It allows you to commit to positive change rather than being mired in guilt or defensiveness. Recognize that growth is a process, and each step you take toward understanding and improving your behavior is a step toward becoming the best version of yourself. This mindset fosters resilience and encourages a proactive approach to personal development.

Cultivating Self-Awareness: Daily Practices

Self-awareness is like a compass guiding you through the often turbulent seas of life. It involves a continuous process of checking in with yourself, much like you might check your phone for messages. Regular self-check-ins help you stay in tune with your emotions and thoughts, allowing you to navigate your day with intention. By setting aside moments to pause and reflect, you create a habit of mindfulness that permeates your daily activities. This mindful presence means fully engaging in the current moment, whether sipping your morning coffee or listening to a friend. It's about noticing what you're feeling and thinking without getting swept away, like observing clouds drift across the sky without trying to change their course.

Incorporating daily habits that enhance self-awareness can transform your relationship with yourself and others. Morning mindfulness practices, such as meditation or deep breathing, set the tone for your day. These practices ground you, helping clear away the mental clutter that accumulates overnight. They provide a moment of stillness before the day's demands take over. Similarly, evening gratitude exercises offer a chance to reflect on your day's experiences. By acknowledging what went well and what you're thankful for, you cultivate a positive mindset that carries you into the next day. These small yet profound practices create a ripple effect that enhances your overall well-being and awareness.

Observing your thoughts and actions is another crucial aspect of cultivating self-awareness. This involves paying attention to your automatic reactions, those knee-jerk responses that occur without conscious thought. By observing these reactions, you can begin to understand the underlying beliefs and emotions driving them. This awareness allows you to pause and choose a different response if needed. Observing your thoughts without judgment is equally essential. It's about noticing your inner dialogue without labeling it good or bad. This practice creates a space to explore your thoughts with curiosity rather than criticism, leading to more compassionate self-understanding.

Integrating newfound insights into daily life is the final piece of the self-awareness puzzle. As you gain clarity about your patterns and behaviors, adjust them to align with your values and intentions. This might involve setting new boundaries in relationships or responding differently in challenging situations. Setting intentions for personal growth creates a roadmap for positive change. These intentions act as guiding stars, helping you stay focused on your goals even when distractions arise. With each adjustment and intention, you reinforce your commitment to living authentically, creating a life that reflects your identity.

In this chapter, we've explored the foundational elements of self-reflection and awareness. These practices are more than tools; they are pathways to understanding yourself better and building healthier relationships. As you continue developing these skills, you'll find that they empower you to navigate life's complexities confidently and empathetically. The next chapter will delve into emotional regulation, examining how we can balance the inner world to foster peace and stability in our daily interactions.

CHAPTER 3
EMOTIONAL REGULATION: BALANCING THE INNER WORLD

Picture yourself standing in a crowded room, a swirl of voices and laughter filling the space. Suddenly, without warning, a wave of emotion crashes over you. It might be anger, sadness, or anxiety, but it hits fast and strong, leaving you feeling out of control. This is the essence of emotional instability—a state where emotions are unpredictable, swinging from one extreme to another without warning. It's like being on a roller coaster, where frequent mood swings make it difficult to maintain emotional equilibrium. One moment, you're laughing, and the next, you're on the brink of tears. This volatility can leave you exhausted and unsure of how to navigate the world around you.

The causes of emotional instability are varied and complex, often rooted in biological, psychological, and environmental factors. Hormonal imbalances, such as those experienced during puberty or due to medical conditions, can significantly impact emotional regulation. These imbalances can heighten sensitivity to stress, making it harder to maintain emotional balance. Stressful life events, whether a significant change like moving to a new city or losing a loved one, can also trigger emotional disruption. These events test your emotional limits, challenging your ability to cope effectively. Psychological factors, such as trauma or underlying mental health conditions, further complicate the landscape, creating a perfect storm where emotional instability thrives.

Emotional instability doesn't just affect how you feel inside; it spills over into your daily life, impacting your relationships and how you function. In personal relationships, frequent mood swings can strain connections, leaving loved ones unsure how to respond. They might feel like they're walking on eggshells, trying to avoid triggering an adverse reaction. This uncertainty can create distance, eroding trust and intimacy. In professional settings, the challenges are equally daunting. Difficulty maintaining emotional equilibrium can affect your performance, as fluctuations in mood impact focus and decision-making. You might struggle to concentrate on tasks or become overwhelmed by minor setbacks. This can lead to conflicts with colleagues or missed opportunities, as emotional instability clouds your ability to navigate the workplace effectively.

Recognizing personal patterns of emotional instability is a crucial step toward managing it. Keeping an emotional diary can be an invaluable tool in this process. By documenting your emotions throughout the day, you can begin to identify triggers and patterns. Certain situations, like crowded spaces or tight deadlines, consistently provoke a strong emotional response. Noting these triggers helps you anticipate and prepare for them, reducing their impact. Pay attention to your physical responses—like tension in your shoulders or a racing heart—as these can reveal your emotional state. Understanding these patterns empowers you to take proactive steps toward emotional regulation, fostering a greater sense of control and stability in your life.

Interactive Element: Emotional Diary Exercise

Start a daily practice of keeping an emotional diary. Jot down the emotions you experience daily and any notable triggers or physical sensations. Over time, review your entries to uncover patterns or recurrent themes. This exercise will help you better understand your emotional landscape, empowering you to manage your reactions more effectively. By identifying triggers and patterns, you can create strategies to mitigate their impact, improving emotional stability and harmonious relationships.

Mindfulness Techniques for Emotional Control

Imagine standing at the edge of a quiet lake, watching gentle ripples expand across the water's surface. This is what mindfulness feels like—a calm awareness of the present moment, allowing you to notice your thoughts and feelings without getting swept away. Mindfulness is a practice that invites you to be fully present and engage with your surroundings and inner experiences with curiosity and without judgment. It's about accepting your thoughts and emotions as they arise rather than resisting or clinging to them. This acceptance creates space for emotional control as you learn to observe your reactions without acting immediately. Mindfulness is not about emptying the mind but being aware of what fills it, offering a pathway to greater emotional regulation.

Incorporating daily mindfulness practices can significantly enhance your ability to regulate emotions. One effective technique is focused breathing. It's simple yet powerful: sit comfortably, close your eyes, and direct your attention to your breath. Notice the sensation of air entering and leaving your nostrils or the rise and fall of your chest. As thoughts intrude, acknowledge them and gently return your focus to your breath. This practice helps anchor you in the present, reducing anxiety and promoting calm. Another valuable exercise is body scan meditation, where you systematically bring awareness to different parts of your body, noticing sensations without judgment. This practice promotes relaxation and heightens bodily awareness, helping you recognize where you carry stress and tension.

Mindful awareness of emotions involves observing and accepting your feelings as they emerge. When you name your emotions—saying to yourself, "I am feeling anxious" or "I am experiencing joy"—you create a sense of distance that allows you to examine them more objectively. This naming process helps demystify emotions, making them less overwhelming. Practicing non-reactivity is equally crucial. When emotions surge, take a moment to pause and breathe rather than react impulsively. This pause allows you to choose your response with clarity and intention. It's about cultivating a space between stimulus and response, where you can decide how to act rather than being driven by automatic reactions. This practice can transform how you engage with your emotions, leading to more thoughtful and balanced interactions.

Integrating mindfulness into daily routines can profoundly change how you experience life. Mindful eating, for instance, encourages you to savor each bite, paying attention to textures, flavors, and the act of nourishing your body. This practice enhances enjoyment and fosters a healthier relationship with food. Mindful walking is another accessible way to incorporate mindfulness. As you walk, focus on the sensation of your feet touching the ground, the rhythm of your steps, and the sights and sounds around you. This practice transforms a simple walk into a meditative experience, grounding you in the present and reducing stress. By weaving mindfulness into everyday activities, you cultivate a state of presence and awareness that permeates your entire life, allowing you to navigate challenges with greater ease and resilience.

Breaking Free from Emotional Baggage

Picture a backpack filled with stones, each representing a piece of unresolved emotion from your past. This is what carrying emotional baggage feels like. Over time, these stones accumulate, each adding weight, making it more challenging to move forward freely. Emotional baggage is the accumulation of these unresolved emotions, and it profoundly influences your present behaviors and reactions. Imagine an old argument you can't let go of or a childhood fear that still lingers in the background of your mind. These unresolved issues can color your current emotional state, often manifesting as anxiety, self-doubt, or even anger in situations that don't warrant such intense reactions. They can trigger responses that seem outsized, leaving you and those around you puzzled by your reactions.

Identifying and acknowledging this baggage is crucial to lightening your load. It requires a willingness to look inward and face the emotions you've tucked away. Reflective journaling exercises can be a powerful starting point. By writing about your past experiences, you create a space to explore and understand the emotions tied to them. Journaling allows you to articulate feelings that might remain unspoken, clarifying how past events shape your present. Talking through these experiences with a trusted friend can also be invaluable. Sharing your story with someone who listens without judgment provides validation and perspective, helping you see your emotions from a new angle. This acknowledgment is the first step toward healing, transforming vague feelings into tangible issues you can address.

Letting go of emotional baggage is a healing process involving the mind and heart. Visualization techniques can help in releasing these pent-up emotions. Imagine closing your eyes and visualizing each stone in your backpack, gradually letting them fall away. This exercise can provide relief, symbolizing the release of burdens you no longer need to carry. Another effective strategy is engaging in symbolic rituals, such as writing a letter to your past self. Pour your heart into this letter, expressing forgiveness and understanding for the emotions you've held onto. Then, choose a meaningful way to let go of it—perhaps by burning it or tearing it to pieces. These rituals are tangible actions that mark the release of emotional ties, creating a sense of closure and freedom.

The benefits of freeing yourself from emotional baggage are profound. As you release these burdens, you gain improved emotional clarity and stability. Without the weight of past emotions clouding your perspective, you can respond to present situations with greater calm and understanding. This clarity enhances your emotional resilience, allowing you to handle life's ups and downs with steadiness. Additionally, releasing emotional baggage opens up space for joy and presence. You become more attuned to the beauty and possibilities around you, able to engage fully in each moment without the shadow of past hurts holding you back. This newfound capacity for joy fosters more profound connections with others as you approach relationships from a place of authenticity and openness.

As you navigate releasing emotional baggage, remember it is a gradual process. Be patient with yourself and honor each step you take toward healing. It's a journey of self-discovery and empowerment, where you reclaim the parts of yourself hidden beneath layers of past pain. With each layer you shed, you move closer to a version of yourself that is lighter, freer, and more aligned with your true essence. Embrace this process with compassion and curiosity, allowing yourself to grow and transform. You can let go of what no longer serves you, creating space for new experiences and opportunities to flourish.

Developing a Growth Mindset: Embracing Change

Imagine looking at a challenge and seeing it not as a roadblock but as a stepping stone. This is the essence of a growth mindset, a concept that transforms how we perceive difficulties in life. A growth mindset revolves around the belief that personal development is always possible. It's rooted in the idea that our abilities and intelligence are not fixed but can be developed through dedication and hard work. This perspective is crucial in emotional regulation because it empowers you to view setbacks as opportunities for growth rather than impossible barriers. When you embrace this mindset, you find that challenges become less daunting, opening up new pathways for learning and improvement.

Cultivating a growth-oriented perspective involves actively reshaping how you think. One powerful method is to reframe negative thoughts that often cloud our judgment. Instead of seeing a mistake as a failure, consider it a valuable lesson. Ask yourself, "What can I learn from this?" You foster resilience and adaptability by shifting your focus from what went wrong to what can be gained. Practicing gratitude and optimism also nurtures a growth mindset. Start each day by acknowledging something you're grateful for, no matter how small. This habit shifts your focus to the positive aspects of life, encouraging an optimistic outlook. Optimism fuels motivation and encourages perseverance, helping you tackle challenges with renewed energy and creativity.

Change and uncertainty are inevitable parts of life. Embracing them is critical to emotional growth. Often, we resist change because it pulls us from our comfort zones, pushing us into the unknown. However, by accepting life's unpredictability, you begin to see change not as a threat but as an opportunity for transformation. When you learn to thrive amidst change, you open yourself to new experiences and perspectives. This adaptability enhances your emotional resilience, enabling you to navigate life's ups and downs gracefully and confidently. Accepting uncertainty doesn't mean you have to like it, but it does mean acknowledging its presence and finding ways to move forward despite it.

Overcoming barriers to a growth mindset often involves confronting deep-rooted fears and resistance. Fear of failure and rejection is a common hurdle. It's natural to worry about falling short or not being accepted. But what if you viewed failure as a necessary step toward success? Embrace the idea that each failure teaches you something valuable, bringing you one step closer to your goals. This shift in thinking can alleviate the fear of taking risks, encouraging you to step outside your comfort zone. Resistance to new experiences is another obstacle. Sticking with the familiar is easy, but growth occurs when you dare to venture into the unknown. Challenge yourself to try something new, even if it's initially uncomfortable. Whether learning a new skill or meeting new people, these experiences broaden your horizons and enrich your life.

To cultivate a growth mindset, start by setting small, achievable goals. Each time you reach one, you build confidence and reinforce the belief in your ability to grow. Surround yourself with supportive individuals who encourage your efforts and celebrate your successes. Their encouragement can help you stay committed to your growth journey, providing motivation and accountability. Remember, developing a growth mindset is not about perfection but progress. It's about being open to learning and willing to adapt. As you embrace this mindset, you'll find that emotional regulation becomes more manageable, and life's challenges become opportunities for personal and emotional growth.

Strategies for Managing Anger and Stress

Anger and stress are like two sides of the same coin, powerful emotions that can affect your mind and body. Anger is a strong feeling of displeasure or hostility that can bubble up unexpectedly, while stress is your body's response to any demand or challenge. When you experience these emotions, your body activates the fight-or-flight response, a physiological reaction that prepares you to face perceived threats. This response floods your system with adrenaline, causing your heart to race, your muscles to tense, and your mind to become hyper-focused on the source of the threat. In the short term, this can be helpful, sharpening your senses and giving you the energy to deal with immediate challenges. However, when anger and stress persist over time, they can have detrimental effects on your health, contributing to conditions like high blood pressure, anxiety disorders, and depression. Understanding the underlying mechanisms of these emotions can help you manage them more effectively.

Managing anger requires a set of strategies that allow you to cool down before reacting. One effective technique is to take a timeout. When you feel anger rising, pause the situation and step away. This break provides a moment to breathe and regain composure, preventing impulsive reactions you might regret later. During this timeout, engage in deep breathing or listen to calming music to help diffuse the intensity of your emotions. Another approach is expressive writing, where you pour your feelings onto paper. This process can be cathartic, allowing you to articulate emotions that might be difficult to express verbally. Writing helps clarify your thoughts and releases pent-up anger, reducing its hold on you. By externalizing your feelings, you gain perspective, leading to more constructive solutions.

It's important to incorporate practices promoting relaxation and balance to reduce stress. Progressive muscle relaxation is a technique where you tense and slowly relax each muscle group, starting from your toes and working up to your head. This exercise helps release physical tension, calming both mind and body. Prioritizing and delegating tasks is another critical strategy. Often, stress arises from feeling overwhelmed by responsibilities. You reduce the pressure on yourself by identifying what needs immediate attention and what can wait. Delegating tasks to others when appropriate also lightens your load, freeing time for self-care and reflection. These practices not only mitigate stress but also enhance your overall well-being.

Combining anger and stress management techniques can lead to a holistic approach that addresses both emotions. Creating a personalized stress-relief plan involves identifying the best strategies for you and incorporating them into your daily routine. This might include setting aside time each day for activities that relax and rejuvenate you, such as yoga, reading, or spending time in nature. Utilizing apps for guided relaxation can support this process, providing easy access to meditations, breathing exercises, and calming music. These resources can be beneficial in moments of high stress or anger, offering immediate relief and helping you regain control. Integrating these techniques into your life fosters a sense of balance and resilience, equipping you to face challenges with poise and confidence.

Building Resilience: Emotional Strengthening Exercises

Resilience is like a rubber band—your ability to stretch and bounce back when life pulls you in different directions. It helps you recover from setbacks, adapt to change, and keep moving forward even when things get tough. Resilience plays a crucial role in emotional regulation, providing a buffer against the stressors and challenges life throws your way. It encompasses emotional flexibility and adaptability, empowering you to navigate adversity confidently and gracefully. By fostering resilience, you equip yourself with the tools to manage emotions constructively, maintaining balance even in the face of difficulty. This ability to rebound enhances your emotional well-being and strengthens your capacity to thrive despite life's inevitable ups and downs.

To strengthen your emotional resilience, you can engage in various exercises designed to build this vital skill. Self-compassion meditations are a good start. These meditations involve taking moments to be kind to yourself and recognizing that everyone experiences difficulties and setbacks. By practicing self-compassion, you learn to treat yourself with the same understanding and care you would offer a friend. This nurturing mindset reduces self-criticism, fostering a sense of inner peace and emotional stability. Another effective exercise is problem-solving activities. You develop an understanding of agency and confidence by tackling challenges head-on through puzzles or real-life situations. This proactive approach teaches you to view problems as opportunities to learn and grow, enhancing your resilience.

A supportive environment is also essential in building resilience. Surround yourself with a network of positive relationships—people who uplift you, encourage your growth, and provide a safe space to express your feelings. These connections act as a foundation of support, offering guidance and reassurance during difficult times. Seeking mentorship is another valuable strategy. A mentor can provide insights, share experiences, and offer advice, helping you navigate challenges with a fresh perspective. Their wisdom and encouragement can bolster your resilience, reinforcing your belief in overcoming obstacles. By cultivating a supportive environment, you create a safety net that bolsters your resilience, providing strength and comfort when needed.

Resilience shines in action, revealing how you respond to life's challenges. Consider professional setbacks, such as losing a job or facing rejection. These moments can feel overwhelming, but resilience empowers you to see them as temporary hurdles. Maintaining a positive outlook and exploring new opportunities can transform setbacks into stepping stones for future success. Similarly, resilience is vital when facing personal loss or grief. While these experiences are undeniably painful, resilience allows you to process emotions, find meaning, and eventually move forward with renewed purpose. Applying resilience in real-life scenarios demonstrates your capacity to adapt and thrive, even in adversity.

Building resilience is an ongoing process, one that requires commitment and intention. Set resilience goals to guide your growth, identifying specific areas where you wish to strengthen your ability to bounce back. These goals include developing better coping strategies or expanding your support network. Reflecting on past resilient moments can also provide valuable insights. Recall times when you faced challenges and emerged more robust —what strategies did you use? What lessons did you learn? By reflecting on these experiences, you reinforce your belief in your resilience, drawing on past successes to navigate future challenges. The continual growth of resilience ensures that you remain adaptable and resourceful, capable of handling whatever life throws your way.

Consider how resilience bridges emotional regulation and personal growth. It's a skill that enables you to face adversity with courage and composure, transforming challenges into opportunities for development. Strengthening your resilience creates a foundation for a more balanced and fulfilling life. In the upcoming chapters, we will explore how these skills can be applied to improve your relationships and foster deeper connections with others.

CHAPTER 4
COMMUNICATION AND CONNECTION: BUILDING BRIDGES

I magine standing at a busy crossroads, the air filled with the hum of voices, each person trying to make themselves heard above the noise. Amid this chaos, clear communication becomes a beacon, guiding interactions toward understanding and connection. Communication is not just about exchanging words; it's about bridging the gap between people, allowing thoughts and feelings to flow freely. This chapter explores how assertive communication can transform relationships, turning potential conflicts into mutual respect and growth opportunities. It's a journey toward expressing needs and desires with clarity and kindness, ensuring your voice is heard without overshadowing others.

Assertive communication is a skill that harmoniously combines clarity and respect. It involves expressing your thoughts and feelings honestly while valuing the perspectives of others. Unlike aggressive communication, which can come off as confrontational, or passive communication, which often leaves needs unmet, assertiveness thrives on balance. It requires you to communicate your needs clearly and respectfully, creating a dialogue where everyone involved feels valued. This balance is vital in maintaining healthy relationships, as it fosters an environment of mutual understanding and cooperation. By practicing assertiveness, you ensure that your voice contributes positively to the relationship, enhancing communication and connection.

One of the cornerstones of assertive communication is the use of "I" statements. These statements allow you to express your feelings and needs without casting blame. For instance, instead of saying, "You never listen to me," which might provoke defensiveness, you could say, "I feel unheard when I'm interrupted." This shift focuses on your experience, inviting empathy rather than conflict. Maintaining eye contact and an open posture further strengthens your message. Eye contact signals engagement and sincerity, while an open posture conveys receptiveness and confidence. These nonverbal cues enhance your words, creating a comprehensive, transparent, and considerate message.

Transitioning from passive or aggressive tendencies to assertive communication requires awareness and practice. Passive communicators often avoid confrontation, fearing conflict or rejection. They might agree to things they don't want to do, leading to resentment and frustration. On the other hand, aggressive communicators may interrupt or dominate conversations, prioritizing their needs over others. Recognizing these tendencies is the first step toward change. You can consciously choose a more balanced approach by identifying when you tend to shy away from expressing your needs or when you overpower discussions. Assertiveness invites you to express yourself confidently while remaining empathetic to others, creating a space where everyone feels heard and respected.

Consider a scenario where you're negotiating boundaries in a relationship. Perhaps you feel overwhelmed by your partner's expectations and need more personal space. An assertive approach involves calmly expressing your feelings and requesting a change. You might say, "I've noticed I need some time alone to recharge, and I'd like us to discuss how we can make that happen." This statement is clear and respectful, inviting collaboration rather than conflict. In a workplace setting, addressing conflicts assertively can prevent misunderstandings from escalating. Imagine you're part of a team where your ideas are frequently overlooked. Instead of harboring resentment, you could assertively express your need for inclusion by saying, "I value our teamwork, and I feel that my contributions could be more impactful if we considered everyone's ideas equally."

Practicing these techniques improves your communication skills and strengthens your relationships. Assertiveness empowers you to express your authentic self, fostering connections based on honesty and respect. It's about finding the courage to speak your truth while honoring the voices of those around you. Through assertive communication, you build bridges of understanding, turning potential conflicts into opportunities for growth and collaboration. This chapter invites you to embrace assertiveness as a tool for healthier, more fulfilling relationships, where every interaction becomes an opportunity to connect and thrive.

Active Listening: The Key to Empathy

Finding someone who truly listens can feel like discovering a hidden treasure in a world of constant noise. Active listening is a powerful tool that transforms ordinary conversations into meaningful exchanges. It goes beyond just hearing words; it involves entirely focusing on the speaker and giving them your undivided attention. This level of engagement shows respect and care, creating a safe space where honest communication can flourish. When you practice active listening, you reflect on the speaker's words, ensuring you truly understand their message before responding. This act of reflection prevents misunderstandings and builds a foundation of trust and empathy.

To enhance active listening skills, consider incorporating specific techniques into your interactions. Paraphrasing is one such method that involves restating what the speaker has said in your own words. This clarifies your understanding and demonstrates that you are engaged and genuinely interested in their perspective. For instance, if a friend is concerned about work, you might respond, "So, you're feeling overwhelmed by the new responsibilities?" Such responses invite correction if needed and show that you are actively processing their words. Additionally, non-verbal cues like nodding or maintaining eye contact further convey your attentiveness. These subtle gestures affirm the speaker's importance, encouraging them to express themselves openly.

Despite its benefits, active listening can be challenging due to common barriers that interfere with our ability to focus. External and internal distractions often pull our attention away from the speaker. In today's digital age, multitasking is tempting but counterproductive when trying to listen actively. Whether it's a buzzing phone or a wandering mind, these distractions dilute the quality of your engagement. Another significant barrier is prejudgments or biases that cloud your perception of the speaker's message. These preconceived notions can lead to misinterpretations, as you might filter their words through your assumptions instead of hearing them. Recognizing these barriers is crucial to overcoming them, allowing you to engage with sincerity and openness.

To practice active listening, try engaging in role-playing scenarios. These exercises involve taking turns listening to and speaking with a partner, focusing on various topics. As the listener, practice paraphrasing and using non-verbal cues to show engagement. Reflect on the experience afterward, discussing what felt natural or challenging. Another effective practice is listening to a podcast and summarizing its key points. This exercise sharpens your ability to distill information and enhances your focus on the speaker's message. By regularly practicing these techniques, you develop a habit of active listening that enriches your interactions, fostering deeper connections and understanding.

Listening to others is a gift you can offer in every conversation. It transforms the simple act of hearing into a profound exchange of thoughts and emotions. Through active listening, you demonstrate that you value and respect the speaker, creating a space where they feel safe to express themselves. This practice strengthens your relationships and cultivates empathy, allowing you to see the world through others' eyes. As you integrate these skills into your daily life, you'll find that your connections become more authentic and meaningful, enhancing the quality of your interactions and enriching your personal and professional relationships.

Practice Exercise: Active Listening Role-Play

Pair up with a friend or family member and take turns being the speaker and the listener. The speaker chooses a topic they're passionate about, while the listener focuses on paraphrasing and non-verbal cues. After each round, discuss what felt effective and areas for improvement. This exercise builds active listening skills, enhancing your ability to engage empathetically in conversations. Through these practice sessions, you'll develop a greater appreciation for the nuances of communication, empowering you to become a more attentive and empathetic listener in all aspects of your life.

Non-Violent Communication Techniques

Consider a moment when words felt like a gentle bridge, connecting two hearts rather than dividing them. This captures the essence of Non-Violent Communication (NVC), a technique transforming how we interact with others. NVC is rooted in the principle of observing without evaluating. This means looking at situations as they are without attaching our judgments or labels. It's about seeing the facts clearly, like observing the sky without naming its colors. When you can describe a situation without passing judgment, you open the door to understanding. Identifying needs and feelings is the next step, recognizing what emotions and desires are at play. Often, conflicts arise when our needs are not met or understood, leading to feelings of frustration or hurt. By naming these needs and feelings, you invite empathy and create space for connection. This practice requires honesty and vulnerability, but it builds a foundation of mutual respect and compassion.

Practicing NVC involves a structured approach to communication, focusing on clarity and empathy. It begins with expressing observations, describing what you see without judgment. For instance, saying, "I noticed you didn't respond to my message," is an observation, free from interpretation or blame. Next, you express your feelings about the observation, such as, "I felt worried when I didn't hear back from you." This shift from accusation to expression invites understanding rather than defensiveness. Following this, you identify your needs, like, "I need to know that we're communicating effectively." Finally, you make an explicit request, asking, "Could we set a time to discuss this?" This step is crucial as it transforms abstract feelings into actionable requests, providing a roadmap for resolution. By avoiding blame and judgment, you foster an environment where dialogue thrives.

NVC can be applied in various contexts, transforming how we handle conflicts and nurture relationships. In family settings, disagreements can often escalate into arguments. Applying NVC, you might address a heated moment by calmly stating, "I see that our conversation is getting intense, and I feel upset. I need us to talk calmly. Can we take a break and come back to this?" Such an approach de-escalates tension and models respectful communication for others. NVC can strengthen collaboration in the workplace, where team dynamics are crucial. Imagine a situation where a project deadline is missed. Instead of pointing fingers, you might say, "I noticed the deadline was missed, and I feel concerned about our team's progress. I need us to discuss how we can prevent this in the future. Can we brainstorm solutions together?" This fosters a culture of cooperation and shared responsibility.

The benefits of adopting NVC are profound, extending beyond mere words to impact the very fabric of our interactions. By focusing on mutual understanding, NVC reduces conflict and promotes cooperation. When both parties feel heard and valued, solutions that might have been obscured by blame or defensiveness emerge. This collaborative spirit enhances personal or professional relationships, fostering a sense of connection and trust. Moreover, NVC encourages a deeper exploration of our needs and feelings, promoting self-awareness and emotional intelligence. As you practice NVC, you develop the ability to navigate emotions with clarity and empathy, enriching your interactions and relationships.

Expressing Emotions Without Causing Harm

In the vast tapestry of human relationships, the threads of emotion are woven intricately, shaping connections with profound depth. Expressing emotions appropriately is like skillfully playing an instrument. It requires balance, timing, and a deep under-standing of one's emotional landscape. Emotions can fester beneath the surface when suppressed, creating tension and misunderstanding. Imagine a pot of water on the stove—it simmers quietly but eventually boils over without release. The impact of unexpressed emotions is much like that pot, causing unintended harm to relationships as unresolved feelings seep into interactions, sometimes manifesting as resentment or bitterness. Relationships thrive on transparency and honesty; when emotions are acknowledged and expressed constructively, they become bridges rather than barriers.

Healthy emotional expression begins with using language that articulates feelings without casting blame. It's about speaking from the heart, using words that convey your experience rather than accusations. For instance, rather than saying, "You make me angry when you're late," you might express, "I feel frustrated when our plans are delayed." This subtle shift redirects the focus from blame to personal experience, inviting understanding rather than defensiveness. Timing is equally crucial in emotional disclosures. Choosing the right moment can prevent a cascade of misunder-standings. For example, addressing a sensitive topic when both parties are calm and receptive increases the likelihood of a productive conversation. It's about finding that window when emotions can be shared and heard without the interference of heightened tension or distractions.

Managing emotional reactions during communication is a skill that can transform potentially volatile exchanges into mean-ingful dialogue. One practical approach is pausing before responding. This brief moment of reflection allows emotions to settle, providing the clarity needed to respond thoughtfully rather than impulsively. Pressing the pause button gives you control over your emotional response. Deep breathing is another powerful tool. When emotions run high, your body's stress response can take over, clouding judgment and escalating tensions. Focusing on slow, deep breaths, you engage the parasympathetic nervous system, calming the mind and body. This practice helps maintain composure and fosters a more open and empathetic exchange, paving the way for constructive communication.

Consider the scenario of sharing feelings with a partner. You might feel neglected due to their busy schedule, and while the temptation to lash out is strong, expressing your emotions effectively can lead to a deeper understanding. Begin by calmly stating, "I've been feeling a bit sidelined with your work commitments, and I miss our time together." This approach opens the door to a collaborative solution rather than a heated argument. In friendships, addressing grievances can be equally delicate. Suppose a friend frequently cancels plans at the last minute. Instead of harboring frustration, you might say, "I've noticed you've had to cancel our plans lately, and I'm feeling disappointed because I value our time together." Such expressions convey your emotions honestly while respecting the other person's perspective, fostering a dialogue that strengthens rather than strains the bond.

Expressing emotions without causing harm is a dance of vulnerability and strength. It invites you to navigate the intricate communication pathways with grace and authenticity. By embracing these techniques, you cultivate relationships built on trust and mutual respect. Each interaction becomes an opportunity to deepen understanding and connection, transforming potential conflicts into moments of growth and healing. You honor your emotions through mindful expression and create a space where others feel safe sharing theirs. This practice enriches your relationships, infusing them with the warmth and empathy that are the hallmarks of genuine connection.

Overcoming the Fear of Vulnerability

Vulnerability often carries a weight that many of us are reluctant to bear. It's the act of being open, showing our true selves without the armor we've carefully constructed over time. In authentic communication, vulnerability is not a weakness but a profound strength. It involves embracing openness and honesty, allowing others to see us as we are without the masks we wear to protect ourselves. This kind of openness lays the foundation for genuine connection, where interactions are about exchanging words and sharing pieces of our souls. Recognizing vulnerability as a strength rather than a liability can transform how we engage with the world. When we allow ourselves to be vulnerable, we invite others to do the same, creating spaces where trust and understanding flourish.

Yet, embracing vulnerability is often easier said than done. Common fears and barriers are formidable obstacles preventing us from opening up. The fear of judgment and rejection are the biggest concern. There's a persistent worry that showing our true selves will lead to criticism or exclusion. Past experiences of betrayal can also cast long shadows, making us wary of letting our guard down. If we've been hurt before, it's natural to protect our hearts from further pain. These fears are valid, and acknowledging them is a crucial step toward overcoming them. It's about recognizing that while vulnerability carries risks, it offers immense rewards in deeper, more meaningful relationships.

Creating a safe environment for vulnerability is essential to overcome these barriers. Establishing trust and respect is the cornerstone of such an environment. Trust is built through consistency and reliability, showing others we are dependable and sincere. Respect involves honoring each person's dignity and worth and valuing their perspectives even when they differ from our own. Encouraging open dialogue without judgment further nurtures this safe space. It means actively listening without interrupting, offering empathy instead of unsolicited advice, and allowing conversations to unfold naturally without rushing to conclusions. By fostering such an environment, we create a sanctuary where vulnerability is possible and welcomed.

The benefits of embracing vulnerability in relationships are profound. When we open ourselves to others, we invite them to do the same, leading to deepened connections and trust. It's like peeling away the layers of an onion, revealing the core often hidden beneath. This process enhances emotional intimacy and understanding as we learn to see each other not as perfect beings but as perfectly imperfect individuals. In this space, we find acceptance and belonging, knowing that we are valued not despite our flaws but because of them. Vulnerability becomes a bridge that connects us on a deeper level, allowing relationships to flourish in authentic and enriching ways.

Repairing Relationships through Honest Dialogue

Imagine a bridge made of words, each carefully chosen and placed to span the gap between two people. Honest dialogue serves as this bridge, crucial in repairing relationships that misunderstandings or miscommunications have strained. It is the foundation upon which transparency and trust are rebuilt. When we engage in honest conversations, we open the door to mutual understanding, allowing both parties to see beyond assumptions and truly hear each other's perspectives. This transparency acts as a balm, soothing the raw edges of past hurts and creating a safe space for healing. Without it, relationships can stagnate, trapped in unresolved issues and resentments. By fostering open dialogue, you address the immediate concerns and lay the groundwork for a healthier, more resilient connection.

Preparing for an honest conversation requires intention and mindfulness. It's about entering the dialogue with a clear purpose, not to assign blame but to seek understanding and resolution. Before the conversation, take a moment to reflect on what you hope to achieve and how you wish to express your feelings. This preparation helps you approach the discussion calmly, setting a positive tone from the outset. During the conversation, practicing active listening and empathy is paramount. This means fully engaging with the other person's words, acknowledging their feelings, and responding with compassion. By doing so, you validate their experience, making them feel heard and respected. This mutual respect fosters an environment where honesty can thrive, enabling both parties to express their needs without fear of judgment or retaliation.

Navigating difficult discussions is often a delicate dance. It's essential to stay focused on the issue rather than the person involved. This focus helps prevent the conversation from devolving into personal attacks or defensiveness. Instead of assigning blame, frame the discussion around the specific behaviors or situations causing tension. This approach keeps the dialogue constructive, allowing you to address the root of the conflict rather than getting sidetracked by emotions. Finding common ground is also vital. By identifying shared goals or values, you can create a sense of unity and collaboration, working together toward a solution that benefits both parties. This collaborative mindset transforms potential conflicts into opportunities for growth and understanding, strengthening the bond that unites you.

Repairing a relationship is not a one-time event but an ongoing process. Once the initial dialogue has occurred, sustaining the progress made through continuous open communication is essential. Regular check-ins allow for addressing any lingering issues before they escalate, reinforcing the commitment to transparency and growth. These check-ins can be informal, casual conversations that ensure both parties remain aligned and connected. They serve as a reminder that the relationship is a priority, deserving of attention and care. Maintaining this level of openness creates a dynamic where both parties feel comfortable expressing their thoughts and feelings, fostering a resilient and adaptable relationship.

As we conclude this chapter, remember that honest dialogue is a powerful tool for healing and connection. It invites you to approach your relationships with courage and vulnerability, embracing the potential for growth and transformation. Through open communication, you build a foundation of trust and understanding, paving the way for relationships that are not only repaired but enriched. The next chapter will explore how setting boundaries can further protect and nurture these connections, ensuring they remain strong and healthy over time.

CHAPTER 5
SETTING BOUNDARIES: PROTECTING YOUR WELL-BEING

Imagine you're building a fence around your garden. This fence doesn't just keep out pests; it defines where your garden ends and the world begins. Boundaries in our lives serve a similar purpose. They delineate where you end and another person begins, protecting your personal space, emotions, and time. Boundaries are essential for maintaining your well-being and ensuring your relationships are nurturing rather than depleting. They help create a sense of security and control, allowing you to interact with the world on your terms. Yet, many people struggle with setting boundaries, fearing they might seem selfish or unkind. But setting boundaries is an act of self-respect, not an act of aggression.

Let's start by defining what boundaries are. In personal and professional contexts, boundaries can take various forms. Physical boundaries are the most tangible. They represent personal space, ensuring your physical comfort and safety are respected. It's like the invisible bubble around you that dictates how close someone can stand during a conversation or whether they can touch you without permission. Then, there are emotional boundaries, which protect your feelings and emotional energy. They help you decide how much emotional investment you offer others and how much you allow them to affect your emotional state. Time boundaries, on the other hand, ensure that you have control over your schedule. They allow you to allocate time for work, leisure, and rest without being overwhelmed by others' demands.

The purpose of boundaries extends beyond mere protection. They play a vital role in maintaining personal well-being and fostering healthy relationships. When you set boundaries, you protect your mental health, creating a buffer against stress and anxiety. Boundaries clarify what you can and cannot handle, preventing burnout and overload. When you establish clear boundaries, you communicate your needs and limits to others, fostering mutual respect and understanding. This clarity reduces misunderstandings and conflicts, creating a more harmonious environment. Boundaries also help you maintain your self-esteem and self-control as you take charge of your life and interactions. They empower you to prioritize your well-being and make choices that align with your values and goals.

Boundaries come in many forms, each significant in its own way. Material boundaries concern your possessions and resources. They define what belongs to you and how you share or protect it. Whether lending a book or sharing a workspace, material boundaries ensure your belongings are respected. Intellectual boundaries relate to your thoughts and ideas. They safeguard your beliefs and opinions, allowing you to express them freely without fear of ridicule or dismissal. Intellectual boundaries are crucial in environments where diverse perspectives are shared, ensuring everyone's voice is heard and valued. These boundaries create a space for constructive dialogue, where ideas can flourish without judgment.

Recognizing healthy boundaries in practice is essential for

understanding their impact. Healthy boundaries manifest as assertiveness in communication. When you express your needs and limits clearly, you assert your right to personal space and respect. This assertiveness doesn't involve force or aggression but reflects confidence and clarity. Mutual respect is another sign of healthy boundaries. In relationships with healthy boundaries, both parties honor each other's limits and needs. This respect fosters a balanced dynamic where both individuals feel valued and understood. Healthy boundaries also involve saying no when necessary, without guilt or fear. Saying no is a powerful way to protect your time and energy, ensuring you can focus on what truly matters.

Reflection Section: Personal Boundary Assessment

Take a moment to reflect on your current boundaries. Consider different areas of your life—physical, emotional, time, material, and intellectual. Are there areas where your boundaries feel solid and respected? Are there any aspects where you think your boundaries are frequently crossed or unclear? Write your observations in a journal, noting any emerging patterns or insights. This evaluation can help you identify areas for improvement and reinforce the boundaries that support your well-being. By regularly evaluating your boundaries, you empower yourself to make necessary adjustments, strengthening your ability to navigate relationships and responsibilities confidently.

The Consequences of Boundary Violations

Imagine you're at a gathering, and someone persistently invades your personal space, leaving you uncomfortable and tense. This situation reflects a boundary violation, which occurs when personal limits are ignored. Recognizing these violations requires attentiveness to your feelings. Often, you might experience a gut reaction—a sense of unease or tension—that signals something isn't right. Boundary violations can manifest in many forms, such as emotional manipulation or guilt-tripping. It's when someone uses your emotions against you, perhaps by making you feel guilty for prioritizing your needs. These tactics can be subtle, yet they erode your sense of self and autonomy, leaving you questioning your worth and priorities.

The impact of boundary violations on mental health can be profound. When your boundaries are crossed, it can lead to increased anxiety and stress. You might be constantly on edge, worrying about subsequent encounters or conflicts. This heightened alertness drains your energy, making it difficult to focus on daily tasks. Over time, the stress can accumulate, affecting your overall well-being. Feelings of resentment and frustration also build up when boundaries are ignored. You might feel powerless and unheard, leading to a simmering anger that can burst unexpectedly. This emotional turmoil disrupts your peace of mind, making it challenging to find joy and contentment in everyday life.

Boundary violations can significantly disrupt relationship dynamics, eroding trust and respect. When someone repeatedly crosses your boundaries, it sends a message that your needs and feelings are not valued. This disregard creates a rift where trust once flourished. You might find yourself questioning the sincerity of the relationship, wondering if the other person truly cares about you. Over time, this erosion of trust can lead to the development of codependency. In such relationships, one person may become overly reliant on the other's approval or presence, losing sight of their individuality. This imbalance creates a dynamic where one person feels responsible for the other's happiness, often at the expense of their well-being.

Addressing boundary violations is crucial for restoring balance and respect in relationships. The first step is to communicate the impact of the breach. This involves expressing how the crossed boundary made you feel, using clear and direct language. For example, you might say, "When you interrupt me during meetings, I feel undervalued and overlooked." This approach focuses on your experience, avoiding blame while highlighting the issue. Reasserting boundaries with clarity is equally important. Clearly state your boundaries, reinforcing their importance. You might say, "I need time alone after work to recharge." Consistency in asserting these boundaries reinforces their significance, helping the other party understand and respect them.

In situations where boundary violations persist, it might be helpful to seek external support. Conversations with a trusted friend or a mental health professional can provide perspective and guidance on managing the situation. They can offer strategies for maintaining your boundaries, even in challenging circumstances. Remember, setting boundaries is an ongoing process, requiring patience and persistence. It's about creating a foundation of respect and mutual understanding where both parties feel heard and valued. By addressing boundary violations with empathy and clarity, you can foster healthier relationships and protect your well-being, ensuring you engage with the world on your terms.

Techniques for Setting Effective Boundaries

Setting effective boundaries begins with a deep understanding of your limits and needs across various aspects of your life. Reflective exercises can be invaluable for developing this self-awareness.

Take a moment each day to consider situations where you felt overwhelmed or uncomfortable. Ask yourself why these feelings arose and what you could do differently to protect your well-being. This reflection helps you pinpoint where boundaries are necessary. Prioritizing personal values and goals is another crucial step. Consider what truly matters to you—time with family, personal growth, or career advancement. Aligning your boundaries with these priorities ensures that you protect what you hold dear, making it easier to say no to things that don't serve your purpose.

Once you understand your limits, the next step is communicating these boundaries clearly and respectfully to others. This involves using direct language to express your needs. Instead of hinting or hoping others will understand, be explicit about what you require. For instance, if you need uninterrupted time to work, say plainly: "I need this hour without distractions to focus on my project." Setting expectations upfront is equally essential. Before entering a situation where your boundaries might be tested, explain your limits to others involved. This proactive approach prevents misunderstandings and sets a foundation for respect. It can feel daunting at first, but remember, clear communication fosters healthier interactions and relationships.

Enforcing boundaries requires consistency and assertiveness. When you establish a boundary, following through with consequences if it's crossed is crucial. This doesn't mean being harsh or punitive; instead, it's about reinforcing the importance of your limits. If someone continues interrupting your work time despite your request, remind them of your boundary: "I've asked for this time to be distraction-free, and it's important for my focus." Consistency in response reinforces the boundary and discourages future violations. Reinforcing boundaries when challenged is also necessary. Sometimes, those around you might test your limits, either intentionally or unintentionally. Stand firm in your boundaries while remaining calm and respectful. By consistently upholding your boundaries, you teach others to respect them.

Boundaries are not static; they may need to adapt as circumstances change. Recognizing when boundaries require adjustment is part of maintaining their effectiveness. Life is dynamic, and what worked for you last year might not suit your current situation. Perhaps a new job demands more time, necessitating reevaluating your work-life balance. Flexibility in different contexts is vital to maintaining healthy boundaries. Be open to reassessing and modifying your limits as your life evolves. This adaptability ensures that your boundaries continue to serve your best interests, supporting your growth and well-being.

Saying No with Confidence and Compassion

The ability to say no is powerful. It acts as a protective shield for your time and energy, keeping you focused on what truly matters to you. When you confidently say no, you assert your right to prioritize your needs without feeling guilty or selfish. This empowerment through refusal is transformative, allowing you to take control of your life rather than being swept along by others' demands. By saying no, you conserve your resources for the people and activities that align with your values and goals. You are maintaining your boundaries and ensuring your commitments reflect your true priorities.

Developing strategies for confidently and compassionately saying no requires practice and intention. One effective technique is to offer alternatives or compromises when declining a request. For instance, if someone asks you to take on an additional project at work, suggest a colleague with the skills to handle it or propose a later date when you can assist. This approach shows that you value the request but must balance it with your existing commitments. Body Language can also play a significant role in conveying your message. A firm yet friendly tone, steady eye contact, and an open posture can reinforce your words, signaling your confidence and sincerity. These subtle cues help communicate your refusal without leaving room for misinterpretation.

Overcoming the guilt and fear often associated with saying no is ongoing. Many struggle with people-pleasing tendencies, fearing that saying no will disappoint others or harm relationships. It's essential to recognize that saying yes to everything can lead to burnout and resentment, which ultimately does more harm than good. Letting go of the need to please everyone is liberating, allowing you to focus on what genuinely matters to you. Building self-assurance is critical to overcoming these fears. Remind yourself that your needs are valid, and saying no is an act of self-care. The more you practice, the more natural it becomes and the less guilt you will feel.

Consider real-life scenarios where saying no effectively can make a significant difference. Imagine a situation where you're asked to take on extra responsibilities. Politely but firmly declining by explaining your current workload and suggesting a timeline for when you might be available can prevent overwhelm and maintain productivity. Similarly, declining an invitation without guilt is entirely possible in social situations. You might say, "Thank you for inviting me, but I need time to recharge this weekend." Offering a future date to meet up shows you're interested in maintaining the relationship, even if you can't participate right now. These scenarios illustrate that saying no doesn't have to be aggressive or negative; it can be a constructive part of communication.

By integrating these techniques into your interactions, you cultivate an environment where your boundaries are respected and your relationships thrive. You can engage with others on your terms, creating space for meaningful connections and personal growth. Remember, saying no is not about rejection; it's about making choices that honor your values and well-being. Each time you say no with confidence and compassion, you strengthen your resolve to live authentically, prioritizing what truly matters.

Navigating Boundary Challenges with Loved Ones

When it comes to family and friends, setting boundaries can be especially tricky. These are the people closest to you, and with them come expectations and assumptions that might not always align with reality. For instance, family members might assume they have unrestricted access to your time, not realizing the strain it puts on your personal space. Similarly, friends might expect you to drop everything immediately, overlooking your need for solitude or prior commitments. These assumptions can lead to tension and misunderstandings if not addressed. Balancing closeness with independence is another common challenge. You cherish these relationships and want to maintain a strong connection, but you also need space to grow and pursue your interests. This balance requires a delicate dance, where you nurture your bonds while honoring your individuality. It's about finding a rhythm that respects your need for connection and autonomy.

Success in navigating these challenges lies in open and honest communication. This means expressing your needs clearly and listening to the needs of others with empathy. When you communicate openly, you create a foundation of trust where both parties feel heard and valued. It's about having conversations that might be uncomfortable but are necessary for the relationship's health. Establishing mutual understanding is critical. It involves acknowledging the other person's perspective and finding common ground. This mutual understanding fosters a collaborative approach to boundaries, where both parties work together to create a dynamic that respects individual needs. It's like building a bridge where each side meets in the middle, ensuring the connection is solid and supportive. By prioritizing communication and understanding, you create a space where boundaries are not seen as barriers but as facilitators of deeper connection.

Resistance to boundary setting from loved ones is not uncommon. People might react defensively, feeling threatened by the change or fearing the loss of closeness. Handling this resistance requires patience and empathy. Remain firm and consistent in your boundaries, even in the face of pushback. It's important to communicate that your intention is not to distance yourself but to create a healthier dynamic. Use empathy to address their concerns, acknowledging their feelings while reinforcing your needs. For example, if a friend feels hurt by your request for more personal time, express understanding for their feelings and reassure them of your care for the relationship. This approach ensures that your boundaries are respected while maintaining the emotional connection. It's about navigating resistance with compassion, transforming potential conflict into an opportunity for growth and understanding.

Maintaining healthy relationships hinges on the presence of boundaries. They act as the framework that supports respect and mutual care. Reinforcing boundaries with positive interactions is essential. Engage in activities that strengthen your bond, showing appreciation and support for one another. Celebrate small victories and acknowledge each other's efforts to honor boundaries. This positive reinforcement solidifies the boundary as a shared value, enhancing trust and respect. Celebrate relationship growth and respect by recognizing the progress made in establishing boundaries. Reflect on how the relationship has evolved and improved, expressing gratitude for your shared journey. These celebrations affirm the commitment to nurturing a healthy relationship where both parties feel valued and empowered. By prioritizing boundaries as a tool for connection rather than division, you cultivate resilient, respectful, and fulfilling relationships.

Maintaining Boundaries in Professional Settings

Navigating the professional world comes with challenges, and understanding professional boundaries is crucial for maintaining a healthy work environment. Professional boundaries are invisible lines that help separate your work life from your personal life, ensuring you can effectively fulfill your roles and responsibilities without overstepping into personal territory. These boundaries are not just about keeping work and life separate; they also involve respecting the roles and responsibilities of yourself and others. In a workplace where boundaries are respected, everyone knows their duties and limitations, which fosters a culture of mutual respect and efficiency. This separation is vital because it allows you to focus on tasks during work hours and enjoy your time without the stress of work-related issues looming over you.

Setting boundaries with colleagues is a delicate but necessary endeavor. It starts with clarifying your availability and communication preferences. For instance, if you prefer to avoid being contacted after work hours, make this clear to your team. You might say, "I am available to discuss work matters between 9 AM and 5 PM, but I need my evenings to recharge." This transparency helps set expectations and prevents misunderstandings. Addressing boundary violations diplomatically is also essential. If a colleague oversteps, approach the situation calmly and respectfully. I appreciate your enthusiasm but must focus on this task without interruptions. Can we schedule a time to discuss this later?" This approach maintains professionalism and ensures your boundaries are respected without creating unnecessary tension.

Managing workload boundaries is crucial to prevent burnout and maintain productivity. It involves prioritizing tasks and knowing when to delegate responsibilities. If your workload becomes overwhelming, take a step back and assess which tasks need immediate attention and which can be postponed or delegated. Communicate with your supervisor to set realistic expectations. I am currently managing several projects. Could we discuss prioritizing tasks to ensure quality work?" This proactive approach helps you manage your workload more effectively and demonstrates your commitment to delivering high-quality results. By setting these boundaries, you create a work environment that supports your well-being and encourages sustainable productivity.

With the rise of remote work, setting boundaries has become more challenging and necessary. In a remote setting, the lines between work and home can blur, leading to a sense of being "always on." Establishing a dedicated workspace can help create a clear boundary between work and personal life. This could be a specific room or a designated corner of your home where work happens. This physical separation helps signal to your brain that it's time to focus when you're in that space and to relax when you leave it. Setting precise work hours and breaks is equally important. Define when your workday starts and ends, and stick to these times as closely as possible. Communicate these boundaries to your colleagues so they understand your availability. Inform them that you will take breaks at specific times to maintain productivity. This clarity helps prevent work from encroaching on your time and gives you space to recharge.

Remember that maintaining boundaries in professional settings is about protecting yourself and fostering a respectful and productive work environment. By setting, communicating, and upholding these boundaries, you create a space where you can thrive personally and professionally. In the next chapter, we will explore how empathy and emotional growth can further enhance your relationships, building on the foundation of respect and understanding established through practical boundary setting.

CHAPTER 6
EMPATHY AND EMOTIONAL GROWTH: STRENGTHENING RELATIONSHIPS

Imagine a world where every interaction is a bridge to understanding, where stepping into another's shoes feels as natural as slipping into your favorite pair. This is the world empathy seeks to create, a place where emotional connections weave the fabric of our relationships. Empathy is the ability to understand and share the feelings of another honestly. It goes beyond surface-level sympathy, acknowledging another's emotions without engaging with them. While sympathy might offer a comforting pat on the back, empathy sits beside you, feeling the weight of your burden, providing a shared space of emotional resonance. Empathy allows us to connect deeply, fostering relationships that are not only meaningful but transformative.

Cultivating empathy begins with practical techniques that enhance your ability to connect with others on a deeper level. One fundamental practice is perspective-taking. This involves consciously imagining yourself in another person's situation and considering their thoughts, feelings, and motivations. For example, if a friend seems distant, rather than assuming disinterest, feel the pressures they face at work or home. This shift in perspective opens the door to compassion, allowing you to respond with understanding rather than judgment. Active listening with emotional validation is another powerful tool. When you listen actively, you focus entirely on the speaker, absorbing their words and the emotions behind them. This means setting aside distractions, maintaining eye contact, and responding with nods or affirmations. By validating their feelings, you acknowledge their experience, creating a safe space for open dialogue. This practice strengthens your connection and encourages others to express themselves honestly, knowing they are genuinely heard.

Applying empathy in everyday interactions can transform the way we connect. Empathy bridges moments of conflict, allowing us to see beyond our grievances to the heart of another's pain. Consider a disagreement with a sibling. Instead of focusing solely on your perspective, take a moment to understand their viewpoint, acknowledging their feelings and frustrations. This empathetic approach can de-escalate tension, opening the path to resolution and mutual understanding. Supporting friends through active engagement further exemplifies empathy in action. When a friend shares a struggle, be present, offering your full attention and knowledge without rushing to fix or solve it. Sometimes, the most excellent support lies in simply being there, providing a compassionate presence that reassures them they are not alone.

Despite its profound benefits, empathy has challenges. Biases and stereotypes are common obstacles, clouding our ability to see others. These preconceived notions can create barriers, preventing genuine connection. Overcoming them requires a conscious effort to question assumptions and embrace diverse perspectives. This might involve engaging with individuals from different backgrounds, broadening your worldview, and challenging your internalized beliefs. Empathy fatigue presents another hurdle. It occurs when the emotional demands of connecting with others become overwhelming, leading to burnout. Practicing self-care and setting boundaries to protect your emotional well-being is essential to manage this fatigue. Recognize when you need a break, and permit yourself to recharge. Balancing empathy with self-compassion ensures you remain resilient and can offer genuine support without leaving you feeling depleted.

Reflection Section: Empathy Development Exercise

Consider an area in your life where empathy could enhance your interactions. Reflect on a recent conversation where you felt disconnected. What biases might have influenced your perspective? How could perspective-taking have altered the exchange? Jot down your thoughts and commit to applying these insights in your next interaction. By consciously practicing empathy, you enrich your relationships and foster a more compassionate and understanding world. This exercise encourages you to actively engage with empathy, transforming it from a conceptual ideal into a lived experience that shapes your daily life.

Emotional Intelligence: A Skill for Life

Imagine standing in a bustling room filled with chatter and laughter, yet sensing the subtle undercurrent of emotions flowing through the crowd. This awareness is part of emotional intelligence (EI), a skill that enhances our ability to navigate the complex web of human interactions. At its core, emotional intelligence involves self-awareness and self-regulation. Self-awareness allows you to recognize your emotions as they arise, understanding their impact on your thoughts and actions. It's about acknowledging feelings like frustration before they escalate, giving you the power to choose your response.

Conversely, self-regulation involves managing these emotions effectively, ensuring they don't dictate your behavior. This might mean taking a deep breath before responding to criticism or pausing to reflect before deciding. Together, these components create a foundation for emotional stability and resilience.

Social skills and motivation are equally vital facets of emotional intelligence. Social skills enable you to interact harmoniously with others, fostering relationships based on mutual respect and understanding. This involves effective communication, expressing yourself clearly while being receptive to others' perspectives. It's about finding common ground in disagreements and quickly navigating social nuances. Motivation, meanwhile, drives you to pursue goals with enthusiasm and persistence. The inner force propels you forward, even when challenges arise. High emotional intelligence often translates to a deep-seated motivation that relies not solely on external rewards but on personal growth and fulfillment. This intrinsic motivation fuels your ability to inspire and lead, creating a ripple effect that influences those around you.

Assessing your emotional intelligence can provide valuable insights into your interpersonal strengths and areas for growth. Emotional intelligence quizzes are a practical tool that offers a structured approach to evaluating your skills. These quizzes typically explore your ability to identify emotions, manage stress, and empathize. Reflecting on past interactions is another effective method. Consider a recent conflict—how did you handle it? Were you aware of your emotions during the exchange, and how did they influence your actions? Examining these interactions gives you a clearer picture of your emotional intelligence. This reflection highlights areas for improvement and reinforces the skills you're already good at, encouraging continuous personal development.

Improving emotional intelligence requires intentional practice and dedication. Developing an emotional vocabulary is a crucial step. Expanding your emotional glossary allows you to articulate feelings with precision, moving beyond basic descriptors like "happy" or "sad" to more nuanced terms such as "elated" or "disheartened." This precision enhances self-awareness and communication, enabling more profound connections. Practicing emotional regulation techniques is equally important. Techniques like mindfulness meditation or deep breathing can help you manage stress and maintain emotional balance. These practices cultivate a sense of calm, allowing you to respond thoughtfully rather than impulsively. By including these strategies in your daily routine, you gradually enhance your emotional intelligence, equipping yourself to handle life's challenges with greater ease and understanding.

The impact of emotional intelligence extends across both professional and personal realms, influencing how you lead, collaborate, and connect. In professional settings, high EI fosters effective leadership and team dynamics. Leaders with vital emotional intelligence can inspire and motivate their teams, creating an environment of trust and collaboration. They navigate conflicts with grace, finding solutions that respect everyone's needs. This not only boosts team morale but also enhances productivity and innovation. In personal relationships, emotional intelligence is the glue that holds connections together. It allows you to build and maintain fulfilling, resilient relationships grounded in empathy and mutual respect. Whether resolving a disagreement with a partner or supporting a friend through a difficult time, emotional intelligence enables you to engage with authenticity and care, strengthening the bonds that enrich your life.

Overcoming Narcissistic Tendencies

Imagine being in a room full of people where one person constantly draws the conversation back to themselves. They seek praise and validation with every word, leaving little room for others to share their thoughts or feelings. This behavior, characterized by an excessive need for admiration, is a common trait of narcissism. It manifests in various forms, from dominating discussions to dismissing others' achievements. The impact on relationships can be profound. Those on the receiving end often feel undervalued and overlooked, creating a disconnect that can erode trust and intimacy. Additionally, a lack of empathy and understanding is another hallmark of narcissistic behavior. This absence of genuine concern for others' feelings can lead to strained interactions, as selfish individuals may struggle to recognize or validate the emotions of those around them.

The roots of narcissistic tendencies are often traced back to deep-seated insecurity and self-esteem issues. Imagine a child growing up in an environment where love and acceptance were contingent on performance or appearance. These childhood experiences can shape how they view themselves and others, fostering a belief that they must always be the best to be worthy. This environment might encourage emulating behaviors that prioritize self-promotion over genuine connection. Such modeling teaches that admiration is earned through superiority rather than empathy, leading to a skewed understanding of relationships. Over time, these learned behaviors become ingrained, creating intricate patterns to break without conscious effort and self-reflection.

Changing these tendencies requires patience and dedication,

but it is possible with the right strategies. Cultivating humility and gratitude can shift focus away from self-centeredness toward appreciation for others. This might involve taking time daily to acknowledge and thank those around you, recognizing the value they bring to your life. Another powerful tool is engaging in reflective practices that encourage introspection and self-awareness. Journaling can be particularly effective, allowing you to explore your thoughts and behaviors without judgment. You see patterns that need change by writing about your interactions and considering how they affect others. These practices encourage a shift from seeking external validation to finding fulfillment within, paving the way for more authentic connections.

The long-term benefits of reducing narcissistic behaviors are significant. Relationships improve as you foster more profound, meaningful connections rooted in mutual respect and understanding. As you become more attuned to others' needs and emotions, you create an environment where trust can flourish. This shift enhances interpersonal relationships and contributes to self-awareness and personal growth. By letting go of the need for constant admiration, you free yourself to explore your true interests and passions without the constraints of external expectations. This newfound freedom leads to a more fulfilling life, where personal satisfaction and happiness are derived from genuine connections and self-discovery.

The Role of Empathy in Healing Relationships

Empathy can profoundly mend the fractures in our connections with others. Empathy acts as a balm when relationships become strained, soothing the wounds that harsh words and misunderstandings often leave behind. It builds trust, creating a safe space where both parties feel seen and valued. This trust is the foundation upon which reconciliation can occur as both individuals understand each other's perspectives and emotions. Through empathy, we recognize the hurt we might have caused and the courage it takes to forgive and move forward. In this way, empathy facilitates healing and the possibility of a renewed bond.

Communicating empathetically while repairing relationships requires a delicate balance of expression and listening. It's vital to express understanding and validation, letting the other person know their feelings are acknowledged and respected. For instance, saying, "I understand why you felt hurt by what happened," can open a dialogue rooted in empathy. Listening without interruption or judgment is equally essential. It means giving the other person the floor, allowing them to articulate their feelings and experiences fully. This kind of listening fosters an environment where both parties can express themselves honestly, leading to a deeper understanding and connection. In this empathetic space, the seeds of reconciliation are sown, allowing relationships to heal and grow stronger.

Real-life examples abound where empathy has bridged divides and restored harmony. Consider the story of two siblings, estranged by a long-standing argument, who found their way back to each other through empathetic communication. By genuinely listening to each other's grievances and acknowledging the pain caused, they began to unravel years of resentment. Similarly, friendships that seemed beyond repair have been mended when one person took the initiative to empathize with the other's struggles, acknowledging their challenges and offering support. These stories are powerful reminders of empathy's capacity to transform relationships, proving that even the most fractured bonds can be healed with understanding and care.

Creating an empathetic environment in group settings further amplifies empathy's impact. Encouraging open sharing and active listening within a group fosters a culture of respect and inclusivity. Whether in a family meeting or a workplace team, promoting a space where everyone feels comfortable sharing their thoughts and feelings can break down walls of misunderstanding. Empathy-building activities, such as sharing circles or collaborative problem-solving exercises, can enhance this atmosphere. These activities encourage participants to step outside their perspectives and consider others' viewpoints, building a collective empathy that strengthens the group. Empathy becomes a shared value in such environments, enriching interactions and fostering community.

Interactive Element: Group Empathy Exercise

Consider organizing a group empathy exercise. Create a safe space where each member can share a personal story or challenge they've faced. Encourage active listening by asking participants to reflect on what they heard and express understanding and support. This exercise builds empathy within the group and strengthens the bonds between its members, fostering a sense of unity and mutual respect. By engaging in this practice, you cultivate a culture of empathy that extends beyond the exercise, influencing interactions and relationships in everyday life.

Practicing Self-Compassion and Forgiveness

Imagine standing in front of a mirror, seeing your reflection and the layers of your experiences, triumphs, and mistakes. Self-compassion asks you to view this reflection with kindness and understanding, much like you would a dear friend. It involves treating yourself gently when you stumble and acknowledging that imperfection is part of being human. This practice is about more than mere kindness; it's about recognizing our shared humanity. Everyone has struggles, and by acknowledging this, you connect with others on a deeper level, fostering a sense of belonging rather than isolation. Self-compassion becomes a bridge to emotional growth, encouraging you to learn from challenges rather than being defeated by them.

To cultivate self-compassion, consider engaging in exercises designed to nurture this inner kindness. Self-compassion meditations can be particularly powerful. During these meditations, you focus on feelings of warmth and acceptance, directing them toward yourself. Picture a soothing light surrounding you, offering comfort and peace. As you meditate, let this light dissolve self-criticism, replacing it with understanding. Journaling is another effective tool for self-kindness. Dedicate time each day to write about your experiences, focusing on how you responded with compassion. Reflect on moments when you showed yourself understanding instead of judgment. This practice reinforces your commitment to treating yourself with care, gradually shifting your inner dialogue toward positivity and support.

Forgiveness is a profound release, a decision to let go of burdens that weigh down your heart. It's important to distinguish between forgiveness and condoning; forgiving doesn't mean accepting hurtful behavior or allowing it to continue. Instead, it frees you from past grievances, offering emotional liberation. Imagine carrying a heavy stone with you everywhere—it's exhausting. Forgiveness is like setting that stone down, allowing you to move forward unencumbered. The impact of forgiveness on mental health is significant. It reduces stress and anxiety, fostering a sense of peace and well-being. By releasing resentment, you create space for healing and renewal, opening the door to a more positive future.

Practicing forgiveness involves intentional steps toward releasing resentment and embracing peace. Begin by reflecting on the benefits of letting go. Consider how holding onto grudges affects you—does it bring peace or perpetuate pain? Acknowledge forgiveness's freedom and how it can transform your emotional landscape. Creating personal forgiveness rituals can also be helpful. These rituals might involve writing a letter to someone you wish to forgive, expressing your feelings without intending to send it. This act allows you to articulate your emotions, providing closure. Another ritual could involve a symbolic gesture, such as lighting a candle to represent letting go. Through these practices, you reaffirm your commitment to forgiveness, nurturing a sense of inner harmony.

By embracing self-compassion and forgiveness, you embark on a path of personal transformation. These practices encourage you to view yourself and others through a lens of understanding and empathy, fostering deeper connections and emotional resilience. As you cultivate these qualities, you create an environment where healing and growth can flourish within yourself and your relationships with others.

Building Empathetic and Supportive Communities

Communities are the heartbeats of our lives, providing the rhythm that keeps us connected and grounded. They serve as vital sources of support and encouragement, offering a safety net when we face life's inevitable challenges. Within a community, you find people who understand your struggles, celebrate your successes, and stand by you in moments of doubt. This shared support fosters resilience, allowing individuals to draw strength from one another. Moreover, communities offer invaluable opportunities for shared growth and learning. Through collaboration and mutual exchange, you gain new perspectives and insights that enrich your understanding of the world. Whether it's a book club, a volunteer group, or an online forum, being part of a community enhances personal well-being and contributes to a collective sense of belonging.

Creating a nurturing environment within these groups is crucial for fostering empathy. One effective strategy is organizing empathy workshops and discussions. These gatherings provide a platform for participants to explore and express their feelings in a safe and supportive space. Individuals can better understand empathy's role in their lives by engaging in guided activities, such as sharing personal stories or role-playing scenarios. Encouraging inclusive and diverse participation is equally important. Diverse groups bring many experiences and viewpoints, enriching discussions and fostering a culture of openness and acceptance. Inviting people from different backgrounds to join creates a tapestry of perspectives that can challenge assumptions and broaden horizons. This inclusivity strengthens the community and enhances its empathetic capacity, creating a space where everyone feels valued and heard.

Building and maintaining supportive networks is an ongoing endeavor that requires intention and effort. Identifying and reaching out to like-minded individuals forms the foundation of these networks. Seek out those who share your values and interests, whether through community events, social media, or mutual acquaintances. These connections can become the backbone of your support system, providing camaraderie and understanding. Hosting regular gatherings or support groups is another way to sustain these networks. Regular in-person or virtual meetings allow members to reconnect, share experiences, and offer support. These gatherings can range from casual coffee meet-ups to structured group discussions, depending on the preferences and needs of the participants. Maintaining consistent contact reinforces the bonds that hold the community together, ensuring that support remains strong and accessible.

Sustaining and growing empathetic communities over time involves continuous learning and adaptation. As the community evolves, so too should its practices and approaches. Encourage members to share feedback and ideas for improvement, encouraging an environment where innovation and growth are welcomed. This adaptability ensures that the community remains relevant and responsive to the changing needs of its members. Celebrating community successes and milestones is also essential. Acknowledging achievements, whether reaching a group goal or supporting a member through a personal challenge, reinforces the value of the community and its impact. These celebrations can be as simple as a congratulatory message or as elaborate as a group event. Recognizing these moments strengthens the sense of unity and purpose within the community, encouraging continued engagement and commitment.

Reflect on how empathetic communities enrich our lives, offering support, growth, and connection. These communities serve as a testament to the power of empathy and collaboration, reminding us of the strength found in unity. As you engage with your community, consider how you can contribute to its growth and well-being, fostering an environment where empathy thrives. The next chapter will explore how these principles can extend beyond our immediate circles, influencing broader societal interactions and promoting a more compassionate world.

CHAPTER 7

HEALING PAST WOUNDS: MOVING BEYOND TRAUMA

I magine walking through a forest; an invisible backpack weighs down each step. Inside are the memories and feelings from past traumas—events that have left a mark on your heart and mind. You might not realize it, but this burden affects every interaction and decision. Past trauma shapes how you see the world, influencing your emotions and behaviors in ways that can be both subtle and profound. Trauma is the emotional response to distressing events, from significant incidents like natural disasters to personal experiences like breakups. The impact varies, but the common thread is the lingering effect on your mental and emotional health.

Unresolved trauma often manifests in various ways. Psychologically, it can lead to anxiety, depression, or a feeling of being constantly on edge. Physically, it might show up as tension headaches, chronic fatigue, or even unexplained aches. These symptoms are your body's way of signaling that something is wrong. They are cries for attention, urging you to acknowledge and address the underlying issues. Recognizing these manifestations is a crucial step in the healing process. It's like finally seeing the contents of that heavy backpack, allowing you to start unpacking it piece by piece.

Identifying traumatic triggers is another essential aspect of understanding trauma's impact. Triggers are specific stimuli—sounds, sights, smells—that evoke strong emotional reactions. You might be suddenly overwhelmed by anger or sadness, seemingly without cause. These reactions are often linked to past trauma, where the brain associates certain stimuli with previous distress. Patterns of avoidance or hypervigilance are also common. Avoidance might mean steering clear of places or people that remind you of the trauma, while hypervigilance involves being constantly on guard, anticipating danger even in safe environments. Both patterns can limit your life, keeping you from experiences and relationships that could bring joy and connection.

Trauma significantly affects relationship dynamics. Trust issues can arise when you find it difficult to believe in the sincerity or reliability of others. This mistrust can lead to attachment styles characterized by anxiety or avoidance. You might cling to relationships out of fear of abandonment or keep others at a distance to protect yourself from potential pain. Additionally, there's a tendency to reenact past trauma in current relationships. This can mean repeating negative patterns learned from past experiences, such as choosing partners who mirror the behaviors of those who hurt you. Understanding these dynamics is vital for breaking cycles and fostering healthier connections.

Assessing the reach of trauma in your life requires introspection and honesty. Reflective journaling can be a powerful tool in this process. Set aside time to write about past experiences, focusing on how they might influence your present. Consider the emotions and thoughts that surface, and explore how they connect to your daily life. This practice can reveal patterns you weren't aware of, allowing you to address them consciously.

Seeking feedback from trusted friends or therapists can also provide valuable insights. They can offer perspectives that you might be too close to see, helping you understand how trauma affects your interactions and relationships. Their support can be a guiding light, illuminating the path toward healing and growth.

Understanding the influence of past trauma is about acknowledging its presence and impact on your life. It's about recognizing that while trauma has shaped you, it doesn't have to define you. By facing these wounds with courage and compassion, you open the door to healing and transformation.

Techniques for Healing Emotional Wounds

Healing emotional wounds is like tending to a garden that's been neglected for too long. It requires patience, care, and the right tools. One of the most effective methods is Cognitive Behavioral Therapy (CBT). CBT helps you identify and restructure negative thought patterns. Imagine your mind is a tangled knot of thoughts. CBT is like the patient's hands gently unraveling it, allowing you to see each thread. By understanding these thoughts, you can challenge their validity and replace them with healthier ones. This restructuring doesn't happen overnight but can change how you perceive and react to the world with consistent effort.

Another powerful approach is Eye Movement Desensitization and Reprocessing (EMDR). This technique might sound complex, but it's pretty straightforward. EMDR uses guided eye movements to help process and reduce the distress associated with traumatic memories. Think of it as a way to move painful memories from the forefront of your mind to a place where they no longer control you. It's like organizing a messy room: everything is still there, but it's tidier and easier to manage. EMDR can be a transformative experience, helping you regain control and peace.

Beyond therapy, self-help strategies play a crucial role in healing. Mindfulness and meditation are accessible practices that encourage you to live in the present moment. Meditating teaches you to observe your thoughts without judgment, like watching clouds pass by in the sky. This practice can reduce anxiety and increase self-awareness, providing a calm space to process emotions. Art therapy is another creative outlet. Creative expression allows you to communicate feelings that words can't capture, whether painting, drawing, or writing. It's a safe space to explore emotions and find healing through creation.

Building emotional resilience is about fortifying your mind against future setbacks. Positive affirmations and self-talk are simple yet powerful tools. Begin each day by affirming your worth and potential. Like seeds planted in fertile soil, these affirmations grow into a strong foundation of self-belief. A daily gratitude practice can also shift your mindset. You cultivate positivity and resilience by focusing on what you're thankful for. Gratitude is like a lens that highlights the good in your life, making challenges seem more manageable.

Support systems are vital in the healing process. Engaging in support groups connects you with others who understand your experiences. These groups offer a sense of belonging and validation, reminding you that you're not alone. A network of empathetic listeners provides comfort and perspective. They are like the sturdy branches you can lean on when the world's weight feels too heavy. Their support can make all the difference, offering encouragement and insight as you navigate your healing journey.

Interactive Element: Gratitude Journaling Exercise

Set aside a few minutes daily to write down three things you're grateful for. They can be as simple as a warm tea or a supportive conversation with a friend. This practice can transform your outlook, helping you focus on the positive aspects of your life over time. This shift builds resilience and fosters a more profound peace and contentment.

By combining therapeutic approaches, self-help strategies, and support systems, you create a comprehensive toolkit for healing emotional wounds. These methods empower you to process past experiences and build a stronger, more resilient self.

Releasing the Hold of Childhood Experiences

Childhood is when the world seems vast; every experience leaves a mark, shaping who you become. It is during these formative years that the seeds of trauma can be planted, often without you even realizing it. Childhood trauma can take many forms, from neglect to abuse, and it can impact you profoundly. Neglect, for instance, might not always be apparent but can leave a child feeling unseen and unimportant. This can lead to beliefs that you must fend for yourself, impacting how you relate to others. Similarly, abuse may foster feelings of worthlessness or fear, leaving scars that influence how you view the world and yourself long into adulthood. These childhood experiences create a framework through which you interpret life, profoundly affecting your behaviors and choices.

To release the hold of these early traumas, it's essential to engage in intentional practices that nurture healing. One such method is inner child work, which involves reconnecting with the part of yourself that experienced those early wounds. This process can be both enlightening and liberating. Reparenting exercises, where you offer yourself the love and guidance you missed, can also be transformative. Imagine speaking to your younger self with compassion and reassurance, letting them know they are safe and valued. This practice allows you to address unmet needs and heal old wounds.

Writing forgiveness letters to your past self can also be a powerful exercise. It helps you express emotions and release guilt or anger you may have carried for years. By forgiving your younger self, you create space for healing and growth.

Reconstructing childhood narratives is another step toward healing. Often, the stories you tell yourself about your past are colored by limiting beliefs formed during traumatic experiences. These beliefs might include ideas like "I'm not good enough" or "I don't deserve happiness." Challenging these beliefs is crucial. You can do this by identifying their origins and questioning their validity. Once you recognize that these beliefs are not truths, you can begin to rewrite them. Creating empowering life scripts that reflect your true potential and worth is a vital part of this process. It's about crafting a new narrative that aligns with the person you are and the life you want to lead.

Embracing and nurturing your inner child is essential for healing. This involves reconnecting with the sense of wonder and creativity often stifled by trauma. Engaging in play and creativity can be healing tools, allowing one to express and explore emotions in a safe environment. Whether painting, dancing, or playing a game, these activities can bring joy and release. They remind you there is more to life than the burdens you carry and that healing can also be about rediscovering joy. Developing self-compassion and kindness towards yourself is equally important. It means treating yourself with the same care and understanding that you would offer a friend. This kindness is a balm for the soul, helping to soothe wounds and foster a sense of peace and acceptance.

In releasing the hold of childhood experiences, it's essential to recognize that healing is not a linear process. It's filled with ups and downs, and that's okay. What matters is the commitment to taking small steps toward understanding and healing your past. As you engage in these practices, you'll find that the grip of childhood trauma begins to loosen. You'll start to see yourself not as a product of your past but as an individual with the power to shape your future. Embracing your inner child and reconstructing your narratives are acts of courage and love, setting the stage for a life of authenticity and fulfillment.

Transforming Pain into Personal Growth

Pain, while often seen as an unwelcome visitor, holds a unique potential to drive personal growth. Consider it a catalyst that propels you toward a deeper understanding of yourself and the world around you. When faced with adversity, there's an opportunity to learn valuable lessons that might otherwise remain hidden. Though born from struggle, these lessons can illuminate the path to resilience and self-discovery. Through these challenging moments, you find the strength to redefine your boundaries, values, and, ultimately, your life's direction. Instead of being a force that pulls you down, pain can become the push that motivates you to change.

Harnessing this potential involves adopting specific techniques that facilitate growth. One practical approach is goal setting and vision creation. By defining what you wish to achieve, you give yourself a destination amidst the chaos. These goals serve as beacons, guiding your actions and choices. Additionally, reflective journaling allows you to process your experiences and emotions. Writing provides a structured way to explore your thoughts, helping you identify patterns and insights to inform your next steps. You might discover a new passion or a previously unrecognized strength in these written reflections, offering clarity and direction.

Embracing change and adaptation is crucial as you navigate

the aftermath of pain. Change is not just inevitable; it is a necessary component of healing. By welcoming new experiences and challenges, you open the door to personal transformation. Each challenge met and overcome builds your adaptability, allowing you to approach future obstacles with confidence and creativity. Flexibility becomes your ally, helping you easily navigate life's unpredictability. This ability to adapt enhances your resilience and enriches your life with diverse experiences and perspectives.

Real-life stories of transformation can inspire and offer hope. Consider individuals who have faced significant life challenges yet emerged more vital and fulfilled. Countless examples of people who have used their pain as a stepping stone to achieve personal milestones. These stories often involve overcoming adversity, whether recovering from a personal loss, a career setback, or a health issue. Through these experiences, individuals find meaning and purpose, often discovering passions they never knew they had. Their journeys demonstrate that pain is a formidable teacher and a source of profound growth and empowerment.

These narratives remind us that transformation is possible, even in the face of overwhelming odds. They highlight the resilience of the human spirit and the capacity for change. Drawing inspiration from these stories shows that your pain while challenging, can be a gateway to a more prosperous, more meaningful existence. It's a shift in perspective that allows you to see pain not as an endpoint but as a beginning—a catalyst for growth that opens up new possibilities and pathways for personal development.

Breaking the Cycle of Self-Destructive Patterns

Self-destructive behaviors often creep into our lives quietly, manifesting as procrastination and avoidance. You might find yourself putting off important tasks, promising to tackle them tomorrow, yet you need more time to get around. This delay can stem from a fear of facing the task, whether because of potential failure or the overwhelming nature of the work itself. Avoidance becomes a shield, protecting you from the immediate discomfort but ultimately causing more trouble in the long run. Similarly, negative self-talk can be insidious, whispering doubts and criticisms that chip away at your confidence. You might engage in self-sabotage, unconsciously setting yourself up for failure to confirm those negative beliefs. These patterns can become a complex cycle to break free from, yet recognizing them is the first step toward change.

Understanding the root causes of these self-destructive patterns requires a deeper look into your fears and beliefs. Often, a fear of failure lurks beneath the surface, a worry that trying and not succeeding would confirm your deepest insecurities. On the flip side, a fear of success can be equally paralyzing. The idea of achieving your goals might bring daunting expectations and responsibilities. These fears are often tied to deep-seated feelings of unworthiness, a belief that you don't deserve success or happiness. These beliefs can take root early in life, be shaped by experiences, and be reinforced over time. They become a lens through which you view the world, coloring your actions and decisions.

To break free from these cycles, developing healthier coping mechanisms is crucial. One effective strategy is to replace avoidance with action, even if it's just a tiny step. Breaking tasks into manageable pieces can make them less intimidating, helping you overcome procrastination's inertia. Additionally, seeking accountability partners can provide the support and encouragement needed to stay on track. Whether it's a friend, family member, or mentor, having someone to check in with can motivate you to push through self-doubt and take action. They serve as a mirror, reflecting your potential and holding you accountable for your goals.

Building new habits is about creating a foundation of positive, constructive behaviors. Establishing routines and consistency is critical. You make a habit that supports productivity and well-being by setting regular times for specific activities. These routines can anchor you, providing a sense of stability and predictability. Celebrating small victories along the way is equally important. Each achievement, no matter how minor it may seem, is a step forward. Acknowledge and reward yourself for these successes as they build momentum and reinforce your progress. Over time, these small victories accumulate, leading to significant change.

Breaking the cycle of self-destructive patterns is not about striving for perfection but about making conscious, intentional choices that align with your values and goals. It involves patience and self-compassion, recognizing that change takes time and effort. Understanding the root causes and implementing strategies to counteract these patterns creates a pathway to a healthier, more fulfilling life.

Finding Peace and Acceptance in the Present

Acceptance is the gentle art of letting go. It invites you to release the tight grip of control you might have over your life and allows you to embrace what is. This doesn't mean resigning to circumstances but acknowledging reality with peace. When you accept your imperfections and vulnerabilities, you open the door to healing. It's a shift in perspective that transforms flaws into unique traits that make you human. This act of acceptance is liberating; it frees you from the constant battle of trying to be someone you're not. Letting go of the need to control every aspect of your life can feel like a huge weight lifted off your shoulders. It allows you to move through the world calmly and confidently, knowing it's okay not to have all the answers.

Mindfulness is a powerful tool in cultivating present-moment awareness. Mindfulness encourages you to fully engage with the here and now rather than dwelling on the past or worrying about the future. One effective mindfulness practice is mindful breathing. By focusing on each breath, you anchor yourself in the present, allowing thoughts to pass by without judgment. This simple act can bring a profound sense of calm and clarity. Meditation takes this further, providing a dedicated time to quiet the mind and explore inner stillness. Grounding exercises, such as focusing on your senses or feeling the earth beneath your feet, can also help maintain emotional balance. These practices encourage you to pause, take a breath, and reconnect with the present moment, offering a respite from the chaos of daily life.

Engaging in activities that foster inner peace and tranquility can transform your day-to-day experience. Nature has a remarkable ability to soothe the soul. Whether walking in the park or sitting by a stream, spending time outdoors connects you to the world in a grounding way; it reminds you of the beauty and simplicity beyond our busy lives. Yoga and relaxation techniques also promote peace. Yoga, emphasizing movement and breath, helps release physical tension while centering the mind. Relaxation techniques, such as progressive muscle relaxation, guide you to release stress from your body systematically. These practices create an oasis of calm, allowing you to recharge and return to your day with renewed energy.

Living fully in the present moment is a practice of freedom. It involves setting daily intentions for mindfulness, which guide your focus and energy throughout the day. By consciously choosing to be present, you open yourself to the richness of life as it unfolds. Focusing on gratitude and appreciation further enhances this practice. By acknowledging the positives in your life, you cultivate a mindset of abundance rather than scarcity. This shift in focus transforms how you experience each moment, bringing joy and contentment to even the simplest pleasures. Living in the present means letting go of past regrets and future anxieties, allowing you to engage with life more authentically.

Finding peace and acceptance is a journey of self-discovery and growth. It involves embracing the present moment with open arms, accepting yourself fully, and letting go of the past's hold. Incorporating mindfulness and peaceful practices into your life creates a foundation for healing and transformation. As you continue to explore these concepts, you will find that they lead you to a deeper understanding of yourself and the world around you. The path to inner peace is not about avoiding challenges but navigating them with grace and resilience. Doing so makes you more attuned to each moment's beauty and possibilities.

CHAPTER 8
SUSTAINING POSITIVE CHANGE: LONG-TERM STRATEGIES

Imagine your day as a blank canvas waiting for you to paint with new, vibrant habits. Each brushstroke symbolizes an action, and you create a masterpiece of positive change with each deliberate choice. Replacing toxic behaviors with positive habits is not just about removing the old but about consciously choosing something better to fill that space. The goal is to transform the canvas of your life into something colorful and fulfilling, where each habit adds depth and richness to your experiences.

Identifying positive habits starts with recognizing activities that can constructively channel your energy and emotions. Stress, often a catalyst for negative behaviors, can find a healthy outlet through exercise or creative hobbies. Physical activity, like a brisk walk or a dance class, boosts your mood and releases endorphins, your body's natural feel-good chemicals. Alternatively, creative endeavors such as painting, writing, or playing an instrument can be a therapeutic escape, offering a sense of accomplishment and joy. Practicing gratitude is another powerful habit that shifts focus from negativity to appreciation. By regularly acknowledging what you're thankful for, you nurture a mindset that seeks positivity, even in challenging times.

Forming new habits can be understood through the "cue-routine-reward" loop. This model, rooted in behavioral psychology, illustrates how habits are built. A cue triggers a routine, followed by a reward reinforcing the behavior. For instance, the cue might be feeling stressed, the routine could be a short meditation, and the reward is a sense of calm. Understanding this cycle helps in structuring habits that stick. Habit stacking is another effective technique linking a new habit to an existing one. If you enjoy a morning coffee, consider stacking a short gratitude practice onto that routine. Over time, these small shifts accumulate, creating a foundation for lasting change.

Consistency is the backbone of habit formation. It's the thread that ties your efforts together, transforming sporadic attempts into a woven pattern of success. Setting daily or weekly reminders keeps your goals at the forefront of your mind, helping you stay on track. Habit trackers or apps can be beneficial, visually representing your progress. They are motivators and accountability tools, showing you how far you've come. Seeing a streak of completed days can be incredibly satisfying, reinforcing your commitment to change.

Celebrating small wins is an integral part of this journey. Each milestone, no matter how minor it seems, deserves recognition—rewarding yourself for reaching a goal—whether a simple treat or a dedicated time for relaxation—reinforces positive behaviors. Reflecting on your changes and their impact fosters a sense of achievement and motivation to continue. This practice boosts morale and encourages perseverance, reminding you that progress is possible and rewarding.

Interactive Element: Habit Tracker Template

Create a simple habit tracker to visualize your progress. Draw a grid with a column for each day of the week and a row for each habit you want to track. Fill in each square as you complete the habit. At the end of the week, reflect on your achievements and consider any adjustments needed for continued success. This tool will help you maintain focus and celebrate your journey toward positive change.

Embarking on this path with intention and dedication holds the potential for profound transformation. Each step you take towards replacing toxic behaviors with positive habits is a step toward a more fulfilling life. Remember to be patient and kind to yourself as you cultivate these habits. Change takes time, and every effort you make contributes to a healthier, more vibrant existence. Each day is a new opportunity to paint your canvas with choices that reflect the best version of yourself.

Setting Realistic Goals for Personal Development

Imagine standing at the base of a mountain, gazing up at the peak, representing your aspirations. Setting realistic goals is like planning your ascent, ensuring each step is deliberate and achievable. The SMART goals framework is a reliable guide for this journey. Making goals Specific, Measurable, Achievable, Relevant, and Time-bound creates a clear path to success. A specific goal answers what needs to be accomplished and who is responsible. It avoids ambiguity and provides a concrete target. Measurable goals include benchmarks to track progress. This allows you to see how far you've come and what remains. Achievable goals consider your resources and constraints, ensuring they're within reach, not just wishful thinking. Relevance ensures your goals align with broader life objectives, while time-bound goals come with deadlines that keep you accountable. This structured approach transforms ambitions into realities, making the climb to your mountaintop both manageable and motivating.

Breaking down significant goals into manageable steps is crucial. Imagine eating an entire cake in one bite; it's overwhelming and impossible. Similarly, tackling a big goal all at once can lead to burnout. Instead, break it into smaller, actionable tasks. Creating a task list provides clarity and focus, helping you prioritize what needs to be done first. Use project management tools or planners to organize tasks visually, allowing you to track progress and adjust as needed. These tools can be digital apps or simple paper planners, whatever suits your style. Seeing each step before you makes the path more transparent, reducing anxiety and increasing motivation. Each task completed is a step closer to your ultimate goal, providing a sense of accomplishment and momentum.

Aligning your goals with your core values is like setting a compass to true north. It ensures that your efforts lead you to a destination that resonates with who you are. Reflect on your values and priorities. Ask yourself what truly matters and what you hope to achieve in the long run. This reflection helps ensure that your goals support your aspirations and contribute to a fulfilling life. When goals align with your values, they become more meaningful and motivating. You're more likely to stay committed and overcome challenges because the journey resonates with your inner beliefs. This alignment creates a sense of purpose, turning your efforts into a meaningful pursuit rather than just ticking off tasks for the sake of completion.

Monitoring and adjusting goals regularly is essential for staying on track. Life is dynamic, and circumstances can change, requiring flexibility and adaptation. Schedule monthly goal check-ins to evaluate your progress. During these check-ins, assess what's working and what isn't. Adjust your objectives based on feedback and new insights. This process lets you stay responsive to changes, fine-tuning your approach to maximize success. Goals are not set in stone; they should evolve as you grow and learn. You maintain momentum and motivation by being open to adjustments, ensuring your goals remain relevant and achievable. This adaptability is a strength, allowing you to navigate obstacles and seize new opportunities as they arise.

Building a Support Network for Accountability

Creating a supportive network is like constructing a safety net beneath a tightrope walker. It provides reassurance and stability, allowing you to take bold steps toward change without fear of falling. Identifying individuals who can offer this support starts with looking around at those who already understand your goals. Family members who share or respect your aspirations can become allies on this path. They often have seen you at your best and worst and can provide feedback rooted in love and understanding.

Similarly, friends who have their growth aspirations can be invaluable. They understand the drive to improve and can offer encouragement and insights from their experiences. It's about surrounding yourself with people who genuinely want to see you succeed and are willing to hold you accountable constructively.

Forming accountability partnerships can significantly enhance your journey of personal development. These partnerships involve regular check-ins through meetings or calls, where progress and challenges are shared openly. The benefits of these partnerships lie in the mutual support they provide. Knowing that someone else is aware of your goals and is there to cheer you on can make all the difference in maintaining motivation. These partnerships create a space where you can discuss setbacks without judgment and celebrate victories, no matter how small. It's about creating the support and accountability that keeps you moving forward, even when the path gets challenging. The key is openness and willingness to give and receive feedback, fostering a relationship built on trust and mutual growth.

Community groups and forums are another powerful avenue for building support and accountability. Joining these groups connects you with like-minded individuals with similar goals and challenges. Online platforms offer a wealth of resources for shared learning experiences, where you can exchange ideas and strategies with people from diverse backgrounds. Local meet-ups and workshops provide opportunities for skill-building and networking in person. These communities create a sense of belonging, reminding you that you are not alone in pursuing personal development. They offer diverse perspectives and insights that can enrich your understanding and approach. Engaging in these groups allows you to draw strength from the collective energy and knowledge of the community, enhancing your journey.

Professional support can also play a crucial role in your personal growth. Hiring a life coach or mentor provides a structured approach to accountability. These professionals offer expertise and guidance tailored to your individual needs and goals. They help you set and achieve objectives, giving encouragement and support. Therapy or counseling provides another dimension of support, particularly in addressing emotional and psychological challenges. Therapists provide a safe space to explore personal issues and develop strategies for overcoming obstacles. They offer tools and techniques for managing stress, improving relationships, and enhancing overall well-being. Leveraging professional support builds a comprehensive network that addresses all facets of personal development, ensuring you have the resources and guidance needed to succeed.

In this interconnected web of support, you find strength in the collective wisdom and encouragement of those around you. Whether through family, friends, communities, or professionals, building a support network empowers you to take confident steps toward growth, knowing that you have allies ready to catch you if you falter. This network provides accountability and enriches your journey, offering opportunities for learning, reflection, and celebration at every turn.

Embracing Continuous Learning and Growth

Imagine life as an open book, each page a new lesson waiting to be absorbed. Committing to lifelong learning is like turning those pages, always seeking new knowledge and insights. This commitment means embracing opportunities to expand your understanding, whether through online courses or workshops that challenge your current perspectives. Enrolling in such programs broadens your skillset and connects you with others who share your thirst for growth. Reading books on personal development topics can also be transformative. These texts often offer wisdom and guidance that prompt introspection and inspire change. As you immerse yourself in new ideas, you cultivate a mindset that values growth and improvement, fostering a life rich with learning.

Curiosity is the spark that ignites the flame of exploration. It encourages you to look beyond your routine and seek new experiences. Trying new hobbies or activities can open doors to parts of yourself that have remained dormant. You could take up painting and discover a hidden talent, or try your hand at baking and find joy in the creative process. Travel, too, broadens your horizons by exposing you to diverse cultures and ways of life. Each journey offers fresh perspectives and challenges preconceived notions. By stepping out of your comfort zone, you learn to appreciate the richness of the world and the endless possibilities it offers. This openness to exploration keeps life vibrant and full of potential.

Reflective practices are the anchors in the ever-flowing river of learning. Keeping a learning journal can be a powerful tool for capturing insights and lessons from experiences. As you write down thoughts and reflections, you create a record of your growth, a tangible reminder of your progress. Reflecting on lessons learned helps solidify new knowledge and encourages more profound understanding. You might write about a challenging situation and how you navigated it or document the skills you acquired from a recent course. This practice reinforces learning and provides clarity and direction, helping you integrate new insights into your life. By regularly engaging in reflection, you maintain a focus on growth and continue to build on your knowledge base.

Adapting to change is a crucial element of personal growth. Life is unpredictable, and embracing change as an opportunity rather than a threat is a valuable skill. Developing resilience allows you to navigate life transitions with grace and confidence. It means viewing each change as a chance to learn and evolve. When faced with new situations, you can draw on past experiences and the wisdom gained from continuous learning. This adaptability enhances your capacity to cope with challenges and empowers you to seize new opportunities. By remaining open to change, you cultivate a mindset that thrives in diverse environments, enabling you to grow and succeed in a constantly changing world.

Celebrating Progress and Acknowledging Setbacks

Imagine walking through a gallery filled with the milestones of your life. Each piece represents a moment of progress, a testament to your growth and determination. Recognizing achievements is like curating this personal gallery, highlighting the moments that have shaped your journey. Creating a "success wall" can be a tangible way to celebrate your accomplishments. This could be a physical space in your home where you post notes, photos, or small reminders of your achievements. Alternatively, a journal that records milestones offers a private space to reflect on your progress. These practices serve as visual affirmations of your hard work and perseverance, reminding you of your capabilities and fueling your motivation for future endeavors. Whether alone or with loved ones, hosting personal milestone celebrations can add a joyful acknowledgment of your efforts, turning each success into a cherished memory.

Setbacks are inevitable, like unexpected detours on a road trip. They might slow you down, but don't have to derail your progress. Understanding setbacks as part of growth allows you to view them constructively rather than as failures. Each mistake or obstacle provides a learning opportunity to get insights that can guide your future actions. Instead of succumbing to self-criticism, embrace self-compassion. Treat yourself with the same kindness and understanding you would offer a friend in a similar situation. This perspective fosters resilience, encouraging you to pick yourself up and try again. By reframing setbacks as stepping stones, you build the confidence to navigate challenges with greater ease and optimism, knowing that each experience contributes to your overall growth.

Reflecting on both progress and setbacks requires tools that facilitate honest introspection. A SWOT analysis—identifying your Strengths, Weaknesses, Opportunities, and Threats—can effectively evaluate your current situation. Strengths highlight what you excel at, while weaknesses reveal areas for improvement. Opportunities point to potential growth areas; threats identify challenges that might impede your progress. This comprehensive view helps you develop strategies that leverage your strengths and mitigate weaknesses, turning potential threats into opportunities for growth. Regular self-assessment checklists provide another reflection layer, offering a structured approach to tracking your development. You gain clarity and focus by consistently evaluating your progress, allowing you to adjust your goals and strategies as needed.

In the face of challenges, building resilience becomes crucial. Resilience is like a muscle; the more you use it, the stronger it becomes. Developing coping strategies for stress can enhance your ability to bounce back from setbacks. Techniques such as deep breathing, meditation, or physical activity can provide immediate relief, helping you regain composure and clarity. Seeking support during difficult times is equally important. Whether through friends, family, or professional guidance, having a network to lean on can provide comfort and perspective. These connections remind you you're not alone, offering emotional support and practical advice. Embracing resilience enables you to face adversity with courage and determination, knowing that each challenge is an opportunity to grow stronger and wiser.

Creating a Vision for a Healthier, Happier Future

Creating a vision for your future is like crafting a roadmap to guide you toward your desired life. It starts with vision-crafting techniques that help you articulate and visualize your aspirations. One effective method is using vision boards. Gather images, words, and affirmations that resonate with your goals and dreams and arrange them on a board. This visual representation is a daily reminder of what you're striving for, keeping your intentions clear and focused. Another powerful exercise is writing letters to your future self. In these letters, express your hopes, dreams, and the person you aim to become. Describe the life you envision in detail, capturing the essence of your aspirations. This process clarifies your vision and sets a positive tone for your journey. Both techniques are about making your dreams tangible, transforming abstract desires into something you can see and feel.

Aligning your vision with personal development goals ensures that every step you take contributes to building the future you imagine. It's about creating harmony between what you want and your actions to get there. Visualize the steps needed to achieve your vision, breaking them into actionable goals. Each goal should be a building block, bringing you closer to your desired future. This alignment keeps you grounded, reminding you of your purpose and preventing you from veering off course. As you set goals, ask yourself how they fit into your larger vision. Are they moving you in the direction you want to go? Are they helping you become the person you aspire to be? This reflection ensures that your efforts are productive and meaningful, guiding you toward a future that aligns with your deepest values and desires.

Regular review and revision of your vision are crucial to keeping it relevant and reflective of your growth. Life is dynamic, and as you evolve, so should your vision. Consider setting aside time for annual vision-setting retreats or sessions. These dedicated periods offer space to reflect on how your vision has changed and what adjustments are needed. Your priorities may shift as you grow and learn, requiring a fresh perspective on your goals and aspirations. This review process is not about discarding your past vision but refining it to fit your current reality. It's about acknowledging your growth and embracing new possibilities, ensuring that your vision remains an inspiring and accurate reflection of who you are and who you are becoming. Regular adjustments keep your vision alive, vibrant, and aligned with your journey.

Living your vision daily involves integrating it into your everyday actions and mindset. Start by setting daily intentions that reflect your vision. These intentions act as guiding lights, helping you stay focused on what's important. They remind you of your larger purpose, keeping you aligned with your vision despite daily distractions. Practicing gratitude for your progress is another vital aspect of living your vision. Celebrate the steps you've taken, no matter how small, and acknowledge the growth you've achieved. Gratitude shifts your focus from what's lacking to what's abundant, fostering a positive mindset that fuels further progress. By aligning your actions with your vision, you create a life that reflects your aspirations, transforming dreams into reality through deliberate and mindful living.

CONCLUSION

I want to reflect on your path through this book as we end this journey together. You've embarked on a transformative exploration, moving from understanding the roots of toxic behaviors to learning actionable strategies for fostering positive change in your life and relationships. Your commitment to this process is a testament to your courage and dedication to growth.

Throughout our time together, you've delved into the importance of self-awareness, realizing how crucial it is to understand your behaviors and patterns. You've explored emotional regulation, learning to balance your inner world and respond to life's challenges with composure. Communication has emerged as a cornerstone of healthy relationships, where expressing oneself assertively and practicing active listening can bridge gaps and build stronger connections. The art of setting boundaries has empowered you to protect your well-being, ensuring that your needs are respected in both personal and professional spheres.

Empathy and healing from past traumas have been pivotal themes, encouraging you to cultivate compassion for yourself and others. By understanding the impact of past wounds, you've taken steps toward releasing their hold and embracing the potential for a brighter future. Each chapter has offered core takeaways, guiding you toward a renewed sense of self and healthier interactions.

I want to celebrate your progress and acknowledge your immense effort. Change is difficult, but you've determined to take these critical steps. Whether big or small, every effort counts. You've embarked on this journey with an open heart, and for that, I commend you. Remember to appreciate your achievements and allow yourself to revel in your progress.

As you move forward, I encourage you to apply the insights and strategies you've learned actively. Continue practicing the tools provided and remain committed to your personal development. Change is a dynamic process, and your growth potential is limitless. Embrace the idea of lifelong learning and self-improvement, recognizing that every day offers opportunities for positive change.

To sustain your growth, consider joining support groups or seeking further learning opportunities. Engaging with community resources can provide additional encouragement and keep you aligned with your goals. These connections can offer support and inspiration as you continue your journey toward healthier relationships.

I am writing to express my deepest gratitude to you for allowing me to be a part of your growth journey. Your trust and willingness to explore these concepts mean the world to me. As you continue on this path, know that you are not alone. I am here to support and encourage you every step of the way.

I leave you with a hopeful and empowering message as we part ways. The journey to a healthier, more fulfilling life is within your reach. You can create positive and lasting change by consistently applying this book's teachings. Embrace your journey with optimism and resilience, knowing that each step forward brings you closer to your desired life and relationships.

May your path be filled with growth, understanding, and joy. You have the strength to transform your life, and I believe in your ability to achieve the happiness and fulfillment you seek. Here's to a future bright with promise and possibility.

REFERENCES

Ackerman, C. E. (2021). *87 self-reflection questions for introspection [+Exercises].* Positive Psychology. https://positivepsychology.com/introspection-self-reflection/

Ackerman, C. E. (2021). *How are habits formed? The psychology of habit formation.* Positive Psychology. https://positivepsychology.com/how-habits-are-formed/#:~:text=For%20an%20activity%20to%20become,favorite%20%E2%80%9Cfeel%20good%E2%80%9D%20neurochemicals.

Ackerman, C. E. (2021). *How to develop empathy: 10 exercises & worksheets.* Positive Psychology. https://positivepsychology.com/empathy-worksheets/

Ackerman, C. E. (2021). *Inner child healing: 35 practical tools for growing beyond childhood wounds.* Positive Psychology. https://positivepsychology.com/inner-child-healing/

Atlassian. (n.d.). *How to write SMART goals (with examples).* https://www.atlassian.com/blog/productivity/how-to-write-smart-goals

Beresin, E. V. (2016, August 24). *8 traits the most toxic people in your life share.* Psychology Today. https://www.psychologytoday.com/us/blog/in-flux/201608/8-traits-the-most-toxic-people-in-your-life-share

BetterUp. (n.d.). *Emotional triggers: What they are and 9 tips to deal with them.* https://www.betterup.com/blog/triggers

Boulder Crest Foundation. (n.d.). *Posttraumatic growth (PTG) – Stories of strength.* Boulder Crest. https://bouldercrest.org/our-approach/impact-stories/stories-of-strength-and-hope/

Brown, B. (n.d.). *Brené Brown: Vulnerability is the key to unlocking intimacy.* Oprah.com. https://www.oprah.com/own-super-soul-sunday/brene-brown-why-being-vulnerable-is-the-key-to-unlocking-intimacy

Burgo, J. (2018, February 7). *7 steps to changing your narcissistic responses.* Psychology Today. https://www.psychologytoday.com/us/blog/understanding-narcissism/201802/7-steps-changing-your-narcissistic-responses

Coursera. (n.d.). *Assertive communication: Definition, examples, and tips.* https://www.coursera.org/articles/assertive-communication

Dornbush, E. (2023, September). *Mindfulness and emotional regulation: 5 exercises from a licensed therapist.* Business Insider. https://www.businessinsider.com/mindfulness-and-emotional-regulation-skills-exercises-dysregulation-2023-9

Farber, B. (2023, April 24). *The impact of childhood trauma on adult functioning.*

Psychology Today. https://www.psychologytoday.com/us/blog/understanding-ptsd/202304/the-impact-of-childhood-trauma-on-adult-functioning

Greater Good Science Center. (n.d.). *Five science-backed strategies to build resilience.* Greater Good Science Center, University of California, Berkeley. https://greater good.berkeley.edu/article/item/five_science_backed_strategies_to_build_re silience

Holding Hope Marriage & Family Therapy. (n.d.). *Active listening in relationships: A path to deeper intimacy.* https://holdinghopemft.com/active-listening-a-key-to-deeper-intimacy-and-understanding-in-your-relationship/

How trauma can affect your relationship. (n.d.). Verywell Mind. https://www.verywell mind.com/how-trauma-impacts-relationships-6745693

Institute for Health and Human Potential. (n.d.). *What is emotional intelligence? Daniel Goleman explains.* https://www.ihhp.com/meaning-of-emotional-intelli gence/

Join Candor. (n.d.). *The importance of self-accountability in personal growth.* https:// www.joincandor.com/blog/posts/the-importance-of-self-accountability-in-personal-growth

Kirkham, C. (2023). *How to set healthy boundaries with anyone.* Verywell Health. https://www.verywellhealth.com/setting-boundaries-5208802

Marriage.com. (n.d.). *Emotional baggage - Types, signs and how to deal with it.* https:// www.marriage.com/advice/relationship/emotional-baggage/

Mayo Clinic Staff. (n.d.). *Borderline personality disorder - Symptoms and causes.* Mayo Clinic. https://www.mayoclinic.org/diseases-conditions/borderline-personality-disorder/symptoms-causes/syc-20370237

Murphy, M. (2023). *Assertiveness can improve your relationships.* Verywell Mind. https://www.verywellmind.com/assertiveness-can-improve-your-relationships-7500841

National Academies of Sciences, Engineering, and Medicine. (2016). *Addressing the social and cultural norms that underlie the acceptance of violence.* National Academies Press. https://www.ncbi.nlm.nih.gov/books/NBK493719/

Neff, K. D. (n.d.). *Self-compassion practices: Cultivate inner peace and joy.* Self-Compassion. https://self-compassion.org/self-compassion-practices/

Recognizing and Overcoming Goal Fatigue. (n.d.). https://www.karleneroberts.com/single-post/recognizing-and-overcoming-goal-fatigue

Rafi, Y. (n.d.). *7 practical tips to say 'no' without feeling guilty.* LinkedIn. https://www.linkedin.com/pulse/7-practical-tips-say-without-feeling-guilty-yousuf-rafi

Restorative Counseling. (n.d.). *5 effective trauma therapy methods.* https://rcchicago.org/5-effective-trauma-therapy-methods/

Richardson, S. (2023). *The impact of ignoring boundaries on mental health.* RBHI. https://www.rbhi.net/the-impact-of-ignoring-boundaries-on-mental-health

Rothschild, G. (2020, September 23). *The science behind toxic relationships, and breaking free.* Intuitive Healing NYC. https://www.intuitivehealingnyc.com/blog/2020/9/23/the-science-behind-toxic-relationships-and-breaking-free

Sternberg, S. (2021). *Carol Dweck on how growth mindsets can bear fruit in children and adults.* Association for Psychological Science. https://www.psychologicalscience.org/observer/dweck-growth-mindsets

The Center for Nonviolent Communication | Home of NVC. (n.d.). Center for Nonviolent Communication. https://www.cnvc.org/

Toxic traits: How to identify and overcome them. (n.d.). Professional Leadership Institute. https://professionalleadershipinstitute.com/resources/toxic-traits-how-to-identify-and-overcome-them/

Valè, N., Gandolfi, M., Vignoli, L., Botticelli, A., Posteraro, F., Morone, G., ... Razek, A. (2021). *Electromechanical and robotic devices for gait and balance rehabilitation of children with neurological disability: A systematic review.* Applied Sciences, 11(24), 12061. https://doi.org/10.3390/app112412061

What is shadow work? How to start and benefits. (n.d.). WebMD. https://www.webmd.com/mental-health/shadow-work